USBORNE TRUE STORIES

HEROES

This edition published in 2007 by Usborne Publishing Ltd,
Usborne House, 83-85 Saffron Hill, London
EC1N 8RT, England.
www.usborne.com

A catalogue record for this title is available
from the British Library

Printed in Great Britain

Series editors: Jane Chisholm and Rosie Dickins
Designed by Brian Voakes
Series designer: Mary Cartwright
Cover design by Michael Hill
Illustrations by Peter Ross

USBORNE TRUE STORIES

HEROES

PAUL DOWSWELL

CONTENTS

CONTENTS

Catastrophe at Chernobyl

The long, thin, red and white chimney of Chernobyl nuclear power station towered over the flat, swampy landscape of the Pripyat Marshes. Just over an hour's drive north of the Ukrainian capital of Kiev, the station was constructed in the 1970s, when it was hailed as one of the Soviet Union's greatest scientific achievements. Its four reactors, with two more being built, made it the largest nuclear power station in the world.

The chief engineer at the plant, Nikolai Fomin, assured visitors that the chances of an explosion in this marvel of modern technology were about the same as being hit by a comet. But he was mistaken. Poor design, bad planning and inadequate staff training meant that Chernobyl was a disaster waiting to happen. And happen it did, on April 26, 1986, when the number four reactor exploded.

A nuclear power station makes electricity in a process known as nuclear fission. Energy is created in a reactor, a specially strengthened chamber inside the power station, by splitting the atoms of a substance called uranium. This process gives off invisible rays called radiation, which can be harmful to living things. In humans, for example, radiation can cause burns and cancer, so power stations have to shield their workers and surroundings from these dangerous rays. The explosion at Chernobyl released huge amounts of radiation into the atmosphere. This caused terrible radioactive pollution, especially to the area immediately surrounding it.

Chernobyl's Number Four Reactor

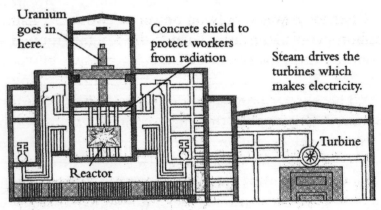

Uranium goes in here.

Concrete shield to protect workers from radiation

Steam drives the turbines which makes electricity.

Turbine

Reactor

Water is heated into steam in the reactor.

Today a huge, ugly, concrete block covers part of the number four reactor. For about 20 miles in all directions, stark branches on dead trees point at the sky, and farmland lies in ruins. In this area of the greatest radioactive pollution, deserted villages and towns slowly crumble and decay, and their empty roads and squares are choked with weeds.

The disaster began on the night of April 25, 1986, when a team of technicians were carrying out routine tests on equipment in the number four reactor. In order to do this, they had to slow the reactor down. Unfortunately, they reduced the reactor's power so much that, like a smoking fire about to go out, it began to shut down.

Chernobyl was supplying power to two and a half million people in nearby Kiev. If the reactor stopped working, the city could be hit by a massive power cut. So the manager on duty that night, Anatoli Dyatlov, ordered workers to restart the reactor, even though doing this when it was so close to shutting down was known to be dangerous.

Control room staff argued that the reactor should be allowed to shut down, which would have been a totally safe procedure. But Dyatlov became enraged at their questioning his decision, and insisted they restart it. He was concerned that he would be held responsible for any loss of power to Kiev, and this might lead to his demotion or even dismissal. Besides, as far as he was concerned, he was just enacting the procedures he had been trained to follow.

Dyatlov's orders were obeyed, but an air of hysteria took hold of the control room as technicians began to grapple with tremendous forces they sensed were running out of control. They were right to feel afraid. As part of the tests, the emergency water cooling system had also been deliberately cut off. In their rising panic, technicians forgot that they had done this, and the reactor began to overheat like a kettle boiling dry.

In the control room, technicians heard a series of ominous thumps, which made the ground tremble beneath their feet. A worker rushed in with the terrifying news that heavy steel covers on the reactor access points were jumping up and down in their sockets.

Then there was a huge thunderclap, the walls shook, and all the lights went out. Dust and smoke billowed in from the corridor, and the ceiling cracked open. A sharp, distinctive smell filled the room, like air after a thunderstorm, only much, much stronger. It was now 1:23am on April 26.

The reactor had disintegrated. It had exploded with such force that it shattered a vast concrete shield, weighing more than a jumbo jet, which lay above the reactor to protect power station workers from radiation. Other equipment, such as a massive fuel machine, had collapsed on top of it.

The reactor just before the explosion

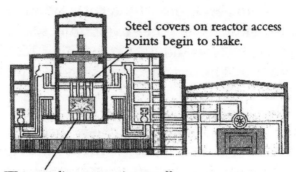

Steel covers on reactor access points begin to shake.

Water cooling system is cut off, causing the reactor to overheat.

The reactor after the explosion

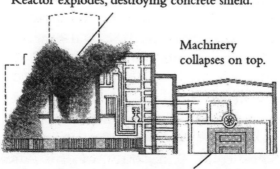

Reactor explodes, destroying concrete shield.

Machinery collapses on top.

Turbine Hall escapes destruction.

Back in the control room, foreman Valeri Perevozchenko's first thoughts were for his colleague Valera Khodemchuk, who he had last seen in the reactor hall. He dashed into the dark corridor, picking his way through clouds of dust and piles of blazing rubble, and made his way to the site of the explosion. The air seemed very thick, and he was also aware of another more sinister sensation. Deadly radiation released by the explosion was passing through him. He could feel it burning his throat, lungs and eyes. His mouth tasted of sour apples.

His blood ran cold and Perevozchenko was seized by panic. He knew that his body was absorbing lethal doses of radiation, but instead of fleeing he stayed to search for his colleague. Peering into the dark through a broken window that overlooked the reactor hall, he could see only a mass of tangled wreckage.

By now he had absorbed so much radiation he felt as if his whole body was on fire. But then he remembered that there were several other men near the explosion who might also be trapped.

Perevozchenko pressed on, running over floors that cracked with the sound of broken glass. He passed a colleague with a radiation monitoring tool, who told him one of his measuring instruments had already burned out, and the one he was using was showing a reading that was completely off the scale.

Still Perevozchenko hurried on into the huge reactor hall. Looking far up to the ceiling, he could dimly see that the roof had been blown off. Firemen summoned to tackle the blaze had already arrived, and their shouts rang across the huge hall. Small fires cast eerie shadows around the mangled mass of pipes and machinery. Streams of water gurgled and splattered from burst pipes. Oddest of all was the strange moaning sound of burning graphite, which was scattered around the floor. This material had come from the very heart of the reactor and was intensely radioactive.

Perevozchenko ran a flashlight over the scene and wondered what on earth he was doing in such a dreadful place. Although he could not see it in the dark, the escaping radiation was rapidly turning his skin brown.

Still, he stopped to listen, in case Khodemchuk was crying for help, then shouted desperately: "Valera! Valera! I've come to rescue you." The echo of his voice died away, and all he could hear was the crackle of the flames and the trickle of running water.

Ahead lay a pile of rubble, and Perevozchenko tore his hands pulling aside concrete and graphite chunks trying to make his way forward. But neither Khodemchuk nor any other colleague was anywhere to be found. Exhausted, he wandered back to the control room, passing the reactor itself on the way. He could see it had been completely destroyed in the explosion and was spewing out deadly radiation.

Perevozchenko knew that his comrades in the control room still believed the reactor was intact, and were struggling to open water vents to try to cool it down. He also realized that the best action to take was to get as many people as possible away from the radiation.

Back in the control room, he struggled to remain conscious. He confronted shift foreman Alexander Akimov and begged him to get everyone to leave the building. But Akimov would not believe the reactor had been destroyed. Perevozchenko's bravery had been in vain. He had not been able to rescue his colleagues, nor warn others to escape before they too became fatally affected by radiation. He was taken to Pripyat Medical Unit and died soon afterwards.

The failure to recognize what had actually happened to the reactor was to cost several more lives, including that of Akimov himself. As he and others struggled to operate valves which would send water to cool a reactor that was no longer there, they too exposed themselves to fatal doses of radiation. Their bodies soon became dark, blistered and swollen, they lapsed into fever and coma and died cruel, painful deaths.

But other workers who endangered their lives had greater success. In the aftermath of the explosion, power station workers in the turbine room were able to drain highly inflammable fuels and gases from storage tanks near to the blazing wreckage. Four received lethal doses of radiation, and another four were hospitalized with painful injuries. But if they had not succeeded, an even greater disaster would have struck Chernobyl. There were another three working reactors at the station. If the fire had spread, these too could have been destroyed, releasing a much greater amount of deadly radiation into the surrounding area.

Unlike poor Valeri Perevozchenko, others who took great risks were able to rescue injured colleagues. Laboratory chief Piotr Palamarchuk and Nikolai Gorbachenko, who were both in the control room at the time of the explosion, began searching for their colleague Vladimir Shashenok. He had been working in a room next to the reactor.

They found him quickly enough, but Shashenok was trapped by a fallen girder and had been badly burned by radiation and scalding steam. They heaved the heavy girder from his body, and carried their injured comrade to the power station infirmary. Palamarchuk and Gorbachenko had exposed themselves to heavy doses of radiation, and they too remained at the infirmary for treatment.

Some of the older staff at the station deliberately chose to carry out the most dangerous tasks to spare their younger colleagues. Alexander Lelechenko, the head of the electrical workshop at Chernobyl, went three times into areas of lethal radiation to disconnect dangerous electrical equipment. Standing next to piles of radioactive rubble, or knee deep in contaminated water, he absorbed enough radiation to kill five people. He stopped briefly to be given first aid for radiation burns, but went immediately back to work for several more hours, only stopping when he was too ill to continue.

Perhaps most of all it was the courage of the Chernobyl firemen that prevented the explosion from causing even worse damage. Lieutenant Vladimir Pravik and his crew dashed to the fire moments after the explosion. Within minutes they were on the roof of the reactor hall, pouring water down on the inferno.

Almost immediately they began to feel sick with radiation poisoning and felt unbearably hot both inside and outside their bodies. But every one of them continued fighting the fire. The roof could collapse at any moment. The tar that lined it was melting, releasing dense toxic smoke and sticking to the firefighters' boots. Radioactive dust fell on their uniforms. One by one they began to falter.

Fire station commander Major Leonid Telyatnikov arrived on the scene soon afterwards. He immediately recognized the scale of the disaster and called out every available fire crew within the area. Telyatnikov issued orders to his men to stand by their posts until the fire had been defeated, and they did not let him down.

For many firemen, fainting and vomiting spells made it impossible to continue but, due to their heroic efforts, the fires caused by the explosion did not spread to Chernobyl's other reactors, and had been extinguished by dawn. The firemen paid a heavy price. Later that day, 17 were taken to a Moscow hospital for specialist treatment.

Treating the injured was Dr. Valentin Belokon. He had been working on the night shift at Pripyat hospital and was called over to Chernobyl shortly after the explosion. As soon as he arrived a guard asked: "Why don't you have special protective clothes?" Belokon realized at once there had been a radiation leak and he was in danger, but as he was the first doctor on the scene he immediately set to work.

He spent all night and all of the next day treating radiation victims, many of whom were very disturbed and near hysteria. By late afternoon of the next day, he too began to suffer from headaches and nausea caused by radiation sickness. He was very much aware of the dangers he faced, but he reasoned: "When people see a man in a white coat, it makes them quieter." He stayed on the site until the next day, when he was too weak to continue working.

By now, the greatest danger was over, but the tragedy still continued to run its course. The nearby town of Pripyat, where most of the Chernobyl workers lived, was completely evacuated. 21,000 people were taken away in convoys of buses, leaving their homes and possessions, never to return. 30,000 had already fled as soon as the disaster happened.

Family pets had to be left behind as large doses of radiation had collected on their fur. Dogs ran behind the convoy until they could keep up no longer and slunk dejectedly back to the empty town. Away from human contact the animals quickly returned to their natural, savage state. Within a day the dogs had formed into packs and hunted down the cats. Within a week they had begun to attack visitors to the town, and teams of soldiers had to be called in to shoot them.

Over a hundred people were taken to hospital after the first night of the disaster. Thirty one of them died over the next few weeks. Some lost their lives because they had tried to rescue injured colleagues. Others died because they had successfully prevented the fire from spreading to the power station's other three reactors. Without their heroism, Chernobyl and the world would have faced a much greater catastrophe.

Afterwards

The Chernobyl accident alerted the world to the fact that a nuclear disaster would never just be a local problem. The immediate area around the explosion became completely uninhabitable, and radiation from Chernobyl even went on to contaminate many other parts of Europe. Traces, for example, were found in Scandinavian salmon and Welsh sheep.

Firefighters and construction crews continued to work at Chernobyl for years after the accident. In the

Map showing how Europe was affected

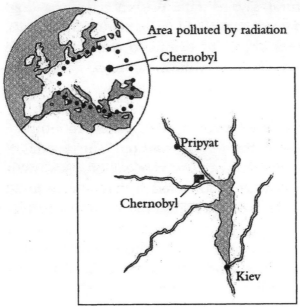

immediate aftermath of the explosion, their main task was to prevent radiation from pouring out of the ruptured reactor. Helicopters flew over, dropping sand and other materials onto it. Eventually a huge concrete casing was built around the site.

At least 116,000 people in the surrounding area had to be rehoused in other parts of the Soviet Union. Although accurate statistics have been difficult to verify, it is thought that around 70,000 people have suffered health problems due to exposure to Chernobyl's radiation leaks.

Today, local scientists are concerned that an earthquake could cause the protective concrete casing around the reactor to collapse, releasing more radiation into the surrounding area. The casing itself is also causing alarm, as it is becoming badly cracked and worn.

The accident has had a positive effect on Russian's nuclear power station industry though. Safety measures and procedures have improved immensely, and there is now a much greater willingness to share ideas with European and American scientists.

12 seconds from death

An icy blast roared through the Skyvan transport plane as the rear door opened to the bright blue sky. On an April morning in 1991, above the flat fields of Cambridgeshire, England, three skydivers were about to make a parachute jump they would never forget.

Richard Maynard was making his first jump. He had paid a substantial fee to plummet from 3,600m (12,000ft), strapped to Mike Smith, a skilled parachute instructor. Expecting this experience (known as a "tandem jump") to be the thrill of a lifetime, Maynard had also commissioned instructor Ronnie O'Brien, to videotape him.

O'Brien leaped backwards from the plane to film Maynard and Smith's exit. The pair plunged down after him, speeding up to 290kmph (180mph) in the first 15 seconds. They soon overtook O'Brien, and Smith released a small drogue parachute to slow them down to a speed where it would be safe to open his main parachute, without it giving them a back-breaking jolt. But here disaster struck. As the chute flew from its container, the cord holding it became entangled around Smith's neck. It pulled tight, strangling him, and he quickly lost consciousness.

Watching from 90m (300ft) above, O'Brien saw the two men spinning out of control, and when the drogue parachute failed to open he knew something had gone terribly wrong. Both men were just 45 seconds from the ground. If O'Brien could not help them, they both faced certain death.

O'Brien changed from the usual spread-eagled posture of a skydiver, and swooped down through the air toward the plummeting pair, with his legs pressed tightly together and arms by his side. He had to judge his descent very carefully. If he overshot, he would have little chance of saving the two men, but this veteran of 2,000 jumps knew what he was doing.

Positioning himself right in front of them, he quickly realized what had happened, and tried to grab hold of Smith so he could release his main parachute. But diving at the same speed was extremely difficult. O'Brien would be within arms length of the falling men and then lurch out of reach. Then suddenly, he fell way below them.

Time was fast running out. The ground was a mere 20 seconds away and O'Brien knew he had only one more chance to save their lives. He spread

How it all happened

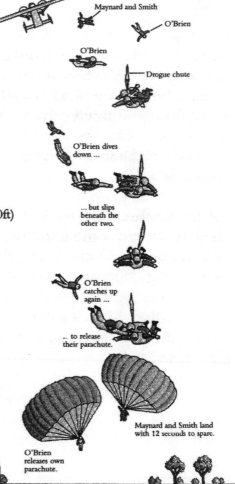

3,600m (12,000ft)
O'Brien jumps from aircraft, followed immediately by Maynard and Smith.

Maynard and Smith

O'Brien

O'Brien

3,000m (10,000ft)
Smith deploys drogue chute which becomes tangled around his neck.

Drogue chute

2,300m (7,500ft)
Smith loses consciousness. O'Brien dives down to help.

O'Brien dives down ...

... but slips beneath the other two.

2,500–1,500m (7,000–5,000ft)
O'Brien catches up with tandem divers but slips underneath them (25 seconds to impact).

O'Brien catches up again ...

900m (3,000ft)
O'Brien catches up again.

700m (2,500ft)
Parachute released (12 seconds to impact). Smith recovers

.. to release their parachute.

650m (2,250ft)
O'Brien deploys own parachute.

Maynard and Smith land with 12 seconds to spare.

O'Brien releases own parachute.

his arms and legs out to slow his descent, and this time managed to connect with the pair. Whirling around and around, O'Brien searched frantically for the handle that would release Smith's parachute.

With barely 12 seconds before they hit the ground, O'Brien found the handle, and the large main chute billowed out above them. Slowed by the chute, Smith and Maynard shot away as O'Brien continued to plunge down. He released his own parachute when he was safely out of the way, a few seconds before he himself would have hit the ground.

By the time the tandem pair had landed, Smith had recovered consciousness, but collapsed almost immediately. Only then did Maynard realize something had gone wrong. Caught up in the excitement of the jump, with adrenaline coursing through his body and the wind roaring in his ears, he had had no idea that anything out of the ordinary had happened.

Odette's ordeal

On a May day in 1943, several German officers sat beneath a cut-glass chandelier in an elegantly decorated room filled with sunlight. The room served as a court at 84 Avenue Foch, Parisian headquarters of the German Gestapo, the Nazi secret police, whose brutal methods were feared throughout Europe.

The court's attention was focused on a bedraggled French woman who sat before them. She had just spent a month in prison, where she had been forbidden to bathe, exercise or change her clothes. Her feet were bandaged where she had been tortured, but she looked far from broken – in fact she seemed to project a curious, detached kind of dignity, as if she were indifferent to her surroundings. Her name was Odette Sansom, housewife turned British spy, and she was on trial for her life.

Odette, who spoke no German, soon became bored, and her eyes wandered around the room. But when the bemedalled colonel who was obviously in charge of the proceedings stood up and read a statement to her, she knew the trial had ended.

She shrugged wearily and told the court she did not speak German. The colonel frowned and explained in halting French that she had been sentenced to death on two counts. One as a British spy, the other as a member of the French Resistance.

Odette looked on the stiff, pompous men before her with scorn, and a giggle rose inside her. "Gentlemen," she said, "you must take your pick of the counts. I can die only once."

Odette had led a life that hardened her to the tribulations she now faced. She was born Odette Brailly, in Amiens, France, in 1912. When she was four, her father had been killed in the First World War. At seven, she caught polio and was blinded for a year, and then spent another year unable to move her limbs. These disabilities turned her into a fiercely independent character. The teenage Odette was remembered as a loyal friend and merciless enemy.

During the First World War, her mother had provided lodgings for English officers. Odette had liked them all immensely, and grew up determined to marry an Englishman. At 19 she did. His name was Roy Sansom. They moved to England in 1932. Odette's years before the Second World War were spent raising three daughters and living the life of an English housewife in Somerset.

War broke out in 1939 and, in less than two years, Nazi Germany had conquered almost all of Europe. When France fell in 1940, it caused Odette much grief. Cut off from her family, she worried constantly about their safety.

In the spring of 1942, Odette heard a government radio broadcast appealing for snapshots of French beaches. An invasion of France from Britain was being planned, and such photos would help decide which beaches were best for landing troops. Odette had spent her childhood by the sea, so wrote to offer her help.

Shortly afterwards an official letter arrived asking her to come up to London. Here she met a man in a shabby back room office, in a building off Oxford Street. They talked for a while and she placed an envelope of her photos on his desk. To Odette's surprise, he pushed them to one side and looked at her closely.

"Actually," he said with a brisk smile, "we're not really interested in your photos. What we'd really like you to do is go to France as a spy."

Odette was flabbergasted.

"Look, I'm a housewife," she said with some exasperation. "I'm not particularly bright and I don't know a thing about spying. I'm sorry. I'll have to say no to you."

"Very well," said the man, who seemed quite unperturbed. "That's quite understandable. But, here, take my number. If you change your mind, just telephone."

Over the next week Odette could not decide what to do. She was torn between her own patriotic feelings for France, and the responsibility she felt for her three children in England. Eventually she decided she would go and train as a spy, and she found a convent boarding school for her daughters. Odette's work was so secret she could not even tell her family and friends what she was doing. She told them instead that she had joined the Army to work as a nurse.

She joined a branch of the British secret service called the Special Operations Executive (SOE), which sent agents overseas. As soon as her training began, the dangers that would face her were made alarmingly clear. "In many ways it's a beastly job," said her commanding officer, Major Buckmaster. "You will be living a gigantic lie for months on end. And if you slip up and get caught, we can do little to save you." In wartime, the fate of a captured spy was almost always execution.

Physical fitness and combat training toughened Odette. She also learned specialized skills, such as which fields were best for aircraft to make secret landings, and how to tell the difference between various kinds of German military uniforms.

Buckmaster had mixed feelings about Odette. He felt she had a temperamental and impulsive nature which could endanger her and any other agents she would work with. "Her main asset is her patriotism and keenness to do something for France," he wrote in a report. "Her main weakness is a complete unwillingness to admit that she could ever be wrong."

In Odette's final days in England, before she went to France, the British secret service made sure her appearance looked as French as possible. She was given a new wardrobe of authentic French clothes, as anything with an English label on it would betray her. But tiny details were taken care of too. The English fillings in her teeth, for example, were taken out and replaced with French ones, and even her wedding ring was replaced with one that had been made in France.

On Odette's last meeting with Major Buckmaster, he supplied her with several different drugs to help with her work. There were sickness pills, energy pills, sleeping pills and, most sinister of all, a brown, pea-sized suicide pill. Buckmaster told her it would kill her in six seconds. "It's rather a horrible going away present," he said, "so I've also brought you this," and gave her a beautiful silver compact.

Odette was flown over to France in November 1942. She began working in Cannes with a group of secret service agents led by a British officer named Peter Churchill. She acted as a courier, delivering money to pay for the work of the Resistance – French men and women who continued to fight the Germans in France even though their country had surrendered. The British secret service worked closely with the Resistance, organizing bands of guerrilla fighters, assisting in sabotage operations and sending back information to England.

Odette picked up stolen maps and documents from the Resistance to pass back to Britain. She found "safe houses" for other spies and suitable locations for aircraft to land with agents or drop weapons by parachute. Peter Churchill was impressed with her. His new agent was quick-thinking, and capable. He thought she was very funny and seemed to possess an unstoppable determination.

Her job was very difficult and danger lurked at every turn. The Germans were constantly arresting

Resistance members, and anyone Odette met in her work could be a double-agent. Eventually the group was betrayed by a traitor named Roger Bardet, who worked for German Military Intelligence – the Abwehr. Churchill and Odette were arrested on April 16, 1943. Even as they were being bundled off at gunpoint, Odette had the presence of mind to hide Churchill's wallet, which contained radio codes and names of other agents, by stuffing it down the side of a car seat on their way to prison.

There was no point denying they were British agents, but Odette spun a complex tale for her captors, hoping at least to save Peter Churchill's life. She said that that they were married to each other, and Churchill was related to the British Prime Minister, Winston Churchill. This was a complete lie. Her "husband", she went on, was an amateur dabbler who had come to France on her insistence. It was she who had led the local resistance ring, and she who should be shot. She told the story so convincingly the Germans swallowed it completely.

A month after their arrest, both of them were taken to Fresnes – a huge jail on the outskirts of Paris. Odette was placed in cell No. 108, and a campaign to break her spirit began. Outside her door a notice read: "No books. No showers. No packages. No exercise. No privileges."

This was where Odette's interrogation by the Abwehr began in earnest. But she also began her own campaign to survive. With a hairpin she carved a calendar on the wall and marked every day. A grate set high in the wall covered an air vent which led to the cell below, and she was able to talk to a fellow prisoner named Michelle. This was a great comfort, as part of her punishment was that she was allowed no contact with other prisoners. Apart from frequent visits to her interrogators, she had no human contact other than an occasional visit by a German priest named Paul Heinerz.

The window in Odette's cell was made of opaque glass. Michelle whispered up to her: "Break that glass pane at once! If you can see even a little blue sky, or the crescent of the Moon, it will be a wonderful sight in your dreary cell. The guards, they'll punish you to be sure. They'll probably stop your food for a few days. It's tasteless slop anyway! Believe me, when you can see outside, you'll feel it's been worth it." Odette didn't think twice.

After two weeks of interrogation, the Abwehr realized their prisoner was not going to tell them anything useful and Odette was taken instead to Gestapo headquarters at 84 Avenue Foch. On her very first visit she was given a large meal. But despite her ravenous hunger, she only ate a little. She knew the meal was intended to make her sleepy and dull-witted.

Her interviewer this time was a sophisticated young man, with Nordic good looks, who smelled of cold baths and eau de Cologne. He was polite, but Odette knew she was dealing with someone who was prepared to be far more brutal than the Abwehr. She was right – this urbane young man was actually a trained torturer. But his questions about Odette's Resistance activity were met with her stock response: "I have nothing to say". The interview came to an end and Odette was returned to Fresnes for the night.

She knew her visit to the Gestapo the next day would be more difficult. The suave young man told her he had run out of patience. Her stomach turned over as a shadowy assistant slipped into the room and stood menacingly behind her. First this man applied a red-hot poker to the small of her back. Still Odette would not talk. Then he removed her toenails one by one.

Throughout this torture Odette gave no cry, although she expected to faint several times. As she was asked the same set of questions, she replied with the same answer: "I have nothing to say."

The young man offered her a cigarette and a cup of tea – a standard tactic by torturers, who hope to catch their victims off guard by showing them unexpected kindness. Although she was in great pain, Odette felt elated. She had kept silent and won her own victory over these inhuman thugs.

Her questioner told her they were now going to remove her fingernails, and Odette's courage wavered. But help came from an unexpected quarter. Just as they were about to start on her hands, another Gestapo man came into the cell. "Ach, stop wasting your time," he said. "You'll get nothing more from this one."

Odette was taken back to her cell at Fresnes, where she bound her injured feet in strips of wet cloth. Then she lay on her cell bed, sick with fear at what the Gestapo would do next. Michelle called throughout the night but she was too weak to answer. Father Heinerz visited. He was so disgusted he could not speak. He kissed her head and left. A few days later, she was summoned to the Gestapo court in the chandeliered ceiling room at Avenue Foch, and sentenced to death.

Returning to her cell after the trial, Odette felt unexpectedly calm. Throughout her torture, she had not betrayed her fellow agents. Most of those she knew were still free to continue their work fighting against the Nazis. Alone on her bunk, she bid a silent good night to each of her three daughters and fell sound asleep. But in the early hours she woke with a start. There was no date for her execution. From now on, every footstep outside her door could turn out to be a guard detachment, arriving to escort her to a firing squad.

Despite this constant threat, Odette was determined not to give up hope. Her story about being related to Prime Minister Churchill had been widely repeated among the prison authorities. Many of the staff who guarded Odette were unusually courteous with her. Like many people in 1943, they had realized the war was going badly for Germany and thought that it would pay to keep on the right side of one of Winston Churchill's "relations".

As summer turned to autumn, Odette fell gravely ill and was moved to a warmer cell. She was also given a job in the prison sewing room and ordered to make German army uniforms. This she refused to do, saying she would make dolls instead. Amazingly, the prison staff let her do this.

Over the winter her health improved but, in May 1944, news came that she was to be transferred to a prison in Germany. As she left, Odette caught sight of one of her interrogators and waved at him gaily, shouting "Goodbye, goodbye." She was determined to let him know he had not broken her spirit.

In the van that took her away were seven other women. They all immediately recognized each other as fellow SOE agents. All instinctively felt they were being taken to Germany to be executed, but they were still delighted to see each other. Their instincts were right. Within a year, all but Odette would be dead.

On the way through Paris, they stopped at Avenue Foch where a Gestapo officer asked if there was anything they wanted. Odette ordered a pot of tea, "... not as it is made in France or Germany, but in the English manner. One spoonful for each person and one for the pot. With milk and sugar please." The tea duly arrived, with china cups and saucers.

Odette was placed on an east-bound train with an armed guard, and spent the next few weeks in several prisons. Once she was presented to a Nazi newspaper reporter who crowed that there were now three Churchills in German prisons, and he was to write a feature on her. Odette dismissed him with a barbed remark, but this was good news. If the Nazis were publicizing her imprisonment, they were hardly likely to execute her immediately.

In July 1944, she was taken to Ravensbrück – a Nazi concentration camp for women on the shore of swampy Lake Fürstenburg. Even the name of the camp, the "Bridge of Ravens", sounded sinister.

Inside its barbed-wire perimeter were row upon row of shabby prisoners' huts, patrolled by guards with whips and savage dogs. All of Ravensbrück's inmates had shaven heads, to cut down on the lice that constantly plagued them. Prisoners who had been there for months or years had been so badly fed they looked like walking skeletons.

Smoke from the camp crematorium constantly filled the sky, scattering a ghastly pall of dust and ashes over the stark, grey interior. The Nazis sent their enemies here to be worked to death and, every morning, those who had died in the night were carried away in crude wooden handcarts. As a young girl walking the cliffs of Normandy, Odette had sometimes wondered where she would die. As she entered Ravensbrück, she felt she knew the answer.

The commandant of the camp, a German officer named Fritz Sühren, was eager to meet Odette.

When she was taken before him, she noticed how clean and well fed he looked. Like most of her captors, Sühren was interested in her connection with Winston Churchill. He ordered her to be placed in "the bunker" — the camp's own solitary confinement cells.

Odette's bunker cell was pitch black and for three months she was kept there in total darkness. But she had been blind for a year of her childhood. She was used to the dark. She passed the time thinking about her three daughters, and how they had grown from babies into young girls. She decided to clothe them in her imagination, stitch by stitch, garment by garment. So completely did she fill her days deciding on the fabric, shades and style of these clothes, that whenever she was visited by camp guards, it seemed like an interruption, rather than the chance to make contact with another human being.

In August, southern France was invaded by French, British and American forces. This was where Odette had done most of her Resistance work. As a spiteful punishment, the guards turned the central heating in her cell to maximum. Odette wrapped herself in a blanket soaked in cold water, but this did not stop her from becoming terribly ill. Near death, she was taken to the camp hospital. It was a strange way to treat someone who had been sentenced to execution. Perhaps the Nazis were still hoping they could break her and she would tell them about her Resistance work.

Away from the bunker, Odette recovered her strength and was returned to her cell. On the way back she found a single leaf that had blown into the treeless camp, and scooped it into her clothing. In her dark world she would trace its spine and shape with her hands, and think about how the wind had blown a seed into the earth which had grown to a tree with leaves and branches that rustled in the wind and basked in the sunlight.

Over the next few months she overheard the execution of several of her fellow agents, all of whom were shot during the winter.

On April 27, 1945, Sühren visited her. He stood at the cell door then drew his finger across his throat. "You'll leave tomorrow morning at six o'clock," he said. Odette wondered if the end had come at last. On April 28 she would be 33. It would be a pity to be shot on her birthday.

When morning came she could hear the chaos that had overtaken the camp. Sühren arrived and bundled her into a large black van with a handful of other inmates. Through the window she could see the guards fleeing from the camp.

The van, together with an escort of SS troops (elite Nazi soldiers), drove west. It soon became clear to Odette that the war was almost over. For the next three days Sühren, his SS escort, and his small band of prisoners, drove from one camp to another as Germany collapsed into anarchy. Many of the prisoners in these camps, so near to freedom but so close to death, were almost hysterical. Some whooped and screamed, making huge bonfires of anything they could find to burn. Others collapsed from hunger, or rushed at their guards only to be gunned down. It all seemed like a delirious nightmare.

On the fourth day away from Ravensbrück, a guard grabbed Odette and dragged her before Sühren. She was told not to bring her few belongings, and was certain she was to be executed. Thrown into Sühren's large staff car, and with an escort of SS guards in two other cars, she sped away from the camp.

After two hours, the three cars stopped by a deserted field and Sühren barked, "Get out." But this was not to be Odette's place of execution. Instead Sühren offered her a sandwich and a glass of wine, and told her he was handing her over to the

Americans. At first she thought this was a cruel joke, but he seemed serious enough. Clearly he thought safely delivering Winston Churchill's relative would get him off to a good start with his captors.

The SS guards spent the next few hours burning incriminating Ravensbrück documents. Then, at 10:00 that night, they drove into a village which had been occupied by American soldiers. Sühren marched up to an officer and said, "This is Frau Churchill. She has been a prisoner. She is a relative of Winston Churchill." He handed Odette his revolver and surrendered.

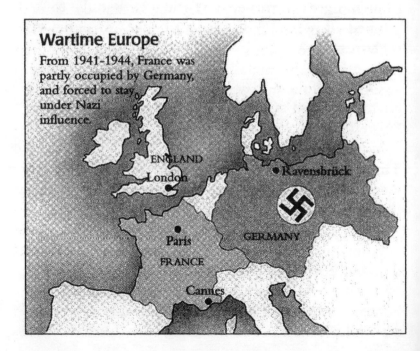

Wartime Europe

From 1941-1944, France was partly occupied by Germany, and forced to stay under Nazi influence.

ENGLAND
London
Ravensbrück
Paris
GERMANY
FRANCE
Cannes

The Americans offered her a place to sleep, but Odette wanted to spend her first night of freedom out in the open. She walked over to Sühren's abandoned open-topped car and sat in the front seat, feeling neither triumph nor elation, just utter exhaustion. Nearby was a party of SS soldiers who had been part of Sühren's escort. One came over and gave her his sheepskin coat to ward off the chill of the night.

To Odette, this act of kindness by a former enemy seemed part of a strange dream, and she expected to wake at any moment and find herself back in the bunker at Ravensbrück. But the dream continued. She nestled into the coat and stared up at the stars. The village clock chimed its quarter hours throughout the night, and it was so quiet she could hear her heart beating.

Afterwards

Following her release, Odette returned to England, after ensuring that Fritz Sühren's American captors were aware that he had been commandant of Ravensbrück. (He was later tried as a war criminal and executed.)

She had several operations on her injured feet before she was able to walk properly again. In 1946, she became the first woman to be given the George Cross, Britain's highest civilian award for bravery, "for courage, endurance and self sacrifice of the highest possible order". She always insisted that the medal had not been given to her personally, but in recognition of the bravery of all French resistance workers.

The medal was stolen a few years later. But following a series of outraged newspaper articles in Britain's national press, it was returned with a letter of apology from the anonymous burglar.

In 1948, after her first husband had died, she married Peter Churchill, the man she had suffered so much to protect. But after eight years they parted, and Odette later married Geoffrey Hallowes, another secret service veteran. In later life she co-founded the British "Woman of the Year" award, worked for charities and spent many hours writing to thousands of people with problems, who had contacted her for advice or inspiration.

Odette Sansom's life as a secret agent was portrayed in the 1950 British film *Odette*, starring Anna Neagle. It was partially shot at Fresnes Prison, Paris, where Odette herself had been held prisoner. She worked as an advisor on the film, but seeing Anna Neagle relive her worst moments was a very painful experience.

She returned to Ravensbrück in 1994, for a ceremony to unveil a plaque commemorating the courage of the British SOE women who had died there. Looking back on the war, Odette wrote: "I am a very ordinary woman, to whom the chance has been given to see human beings at their best and at their worst."

She died in 1995, aged 82.

Helicopter heroes

The situation outlined in an emergency phone call to Royal Naval Air Station Culdrose, Cornwall, UK, was deeply alarming. On October 28, 1989, a huge Pakistani container ship, named *Murree*, was caught in a severe storm some distance from Start Bay, Dartmouth. Her cargo, piled high on the deck, had shifted in the rough weather. One stack of containers had broken free and fallen into the sea. But one of the heavy steel containers swung back against the hull and split it open. Now vast amounts of water were flooding into the hold. A lifeboat had already been launched from nearby Brixham, but the turbulent sea had made docking all but impossible.

So Sea King helicopters were dispatched from Culdrose to help in the rescue operation. They arrived above the *Murree* within minutes, and two Royal Navy divers, Petty Officers Steve Wright and Dave Wallace, were lowered down onto her heaving deck.

Wright and Wallace were disturbed to discover that there were 40 people on board the sinking vessel, including many of the wives and children of the crew. As gale force winds lashed the sloping deck, they gathered together the terrified crew and passengers. With the bow already underwater, they strapped them two at a time into harnesses so they could be lifted into waiting helicopters. But time was running out.

Just as the last two crew members were being winched off the deck, the *Murree* lurched alarmingly and the bow sank deeper beneath the waves. Wright grabbed hold of a nearby deck railing to stop himself from falling. Wallace was not so lucky and slithered down the tilting deck towards the boiling sea below. Fortunately, his leg caught in a coil of rope. This broke his fall, but he had to struggle frantically to break free.

The *Murree* was going down fast. On the stern of the ship the two divers grabbed desperately at the harness from the helicopter overhead, but it slipped from their grip. There was only one thing left to do. Taking a huge leap from the stern into the heaving waves, they plunged deep underwater and surfaced to see the ship's stern towering over them.

Fearing they would be sucked under as the ship went down, the two swam for their lives. Battered by huge waves and debris from the wreckage, they floundered in the sea until a Sea King helicopter was able to pluck them from the water.

Back on dry land, the *Murree*'s Captain Abdul Ajeeq, who had been the last crew member to leave the doomed vessel, told waiting newspaper reporters: "These helicopter men are fantastic. They gave us our lives."

Afterwards

In 1990, Wright and Wallace's courage was officially recognized when they were presented with the George Medal. The *Murree* still lies deep under the water, halfway between Star Point and Alderney in the Channel Islands. It is now almost totally covered in brittlestars and sea anemones, and is occasionally visited by divers interested in exploring its rusting interior.

Punching a hole in the sky

In the summer of 1947, a huge silver B-29 bomber soared off the windswept runway at Muroc airbase, California. As it climbed into a cloudless August sky, the sun gleamed brightly on a strange bullet-shaped craft slung under its belly. This was the Bell X-1 rocket, a machine designed to fly beyond the very frontiers of aviation science.

The X-1's pilot, a 24-year-old US Airforce captain named Chuck Yeager, knew he was dicing with death every time he took to the sky. But before the year was out, Yeager was determined to fly this rocket beyond the speed of sound – faster than any man had ever flown before.

In 1947, supersonic flight – as any aircraft speed faster than sound is known – was dark, forbidding territory. Yeager joked that it might make his ears fall off. But it was true that some aircraft that had attempted to break the sound barrier had literally disintegrated, shaken apart by invisible forces no one yet understood.

Most aviation engineers thought no aircraft could fly faster than sound. They believed there was a "sound barrier" – an invisible wall of turbulence that would tear apart any plane that tried to break through it.

Military pilots rarely flew on such dangerous experimental missions. A highly paid civilian test pilot, named "Slick" Goodlin, had begun the project. As the X-1 tests had approached the speed of sound, he had demanded a $150,000 bonus for an actual attempt on the sound barrier. The US military could no longer afford him, and recruited a pilot from their own ranks.

Despite the obvious dangers, Yeager volunteered. Flying filled him with an indescribable joy. The chance to pilot a beautiful aircraft like the X-1 was heaven sent. Besides, in the competitive world of the test pilot, the opportunity to become the first man to travel faster than sound was too good to miss. He took the job on his standard captain's pay of $283 a month.

With his slow, West Virginian country drawl, Yeager was something of an oddball in the high-powered world of experimental flying. But his exceptional skill, and quick thinking coolness under pressure, made him by far the best test pilot at Muroc.

Lacking a college education, he had joined the US airforce at 18 years old as a mechanic. Yeager had extraordinary hand-eye coordination and excellent eyesight. This was soon noticed and he was transferred to flight-training school. In World War Two, he piloted fighter planes over Europe, was shot down over France and escaped back to his base in England. He flew nearly 100 combat missions, and once shot down five German aircraft in a single day.

Now, as the B-29 climbed into the sky on this breezy August day, Yeager was about to pilot the X-1 on its first powered flight. He had flown the plane before, but only on glide flights. This time it was brimming with liquid oxygen and alcohol fuel.

At the flick of a rocket ignition switch, his craft could shoot straight to the top of the sky, or it could explode into a thousand flaming pieces. He was nervous, but told himself fear was a pilot's friend. It sharpened his senses and kept his mind focused on the job in hand.

Trying to break through the sound barrier was so dangerous it could only be attempted in small stages. The X-1 would be dropped from the bomb bay of the B-29 at 8,000m (25,000ft), and then Yeager would ignite the rockets and fly off into the horizon. Being unleashed from the B-29, rather than taking off in the usual way, saved weight on fuel. The less weight the X-1 carried, the faster it was going to fly.

The Bell X-1

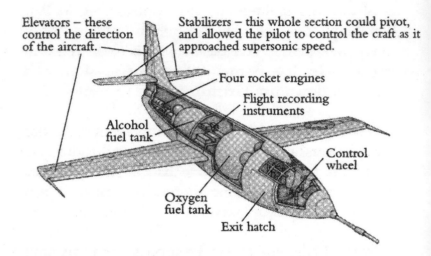

Elevators – these control the direction of the aircraft.

Stabilizers – this whole section could pivot, and allowed the pilot to control the craft as it approached supersonic speed.

Four rocket engines

Flight recording instruments

Alcohol fuel tank

Control wheel

Oxygen fuel tank

Exit hatch

Yeager didn't sit in the X-1 at take-off, in case it accidentally dropped out of the B-29 before they reached a safe height for the rocket to fly. Near the drop zone, he left the B-29's cockpit and squeezed through a narrow corridor to the bomb bay. Here he could see right down to the surface of the Earth.

Yeager had to climb down a ladder to a small metal platform and squeeze feet first through the hatch into his craft. At such a height, it was viciously cold and the wind threatened to tear his frozen fingers from the ladder's metal rungs.

Once he was inside, the door to the hatch was lowered down. His flight engineer and good friend, Jack Ridley, stood on the ladder and held it in place as it was locked from the inside. Yeager trusted his flight engineer with his life. Only 29, Ridley had already established a reputation as a brilliant scientist.

Some people said the X-1 was the most beautiful aircraft ever built. Yeager knew it was certainly the coldest. It was so chilly in the darkened bomb bay that he had to bang his gloved hands together to keep them from becoming numb. The X-1 cockpit had no heating, and directly behind the seat sat several hundred gallons of freezing-cold liquid oxygen fuel; the belly of the craft was now coated in a thin film of ice.

But now was no time to worry about the cold. "All set," radioed in Ridley, back inside the B-29. "You bet," said Yeager. "Let's go to work."

The X-1 dropped like a stone. Yeager was blinded by bright sunlight and wrestled to get his craft under control. When the X-1 was flying level, he flicked the rocket ignition switch on his instrument panel. A luminous jet of flame roared from the rocket exhaust and a huge surge of power slammed him back into his seat. It seemed as if he was heading for the very roof of the sky and was going to punch his way into space itself.

The sound barrier

Mach 0.5
As a plane flies through the air it creates small disturbances, or shock waves, in the air around it.

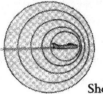

Shock waves

Mach 0.9
Near the sound barrier, shock waves travel at the same speed as the plane, causing buffeting.

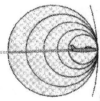

Sound barrier

Mach 1
Above the speed of sound a plane travels faster than the shock waves.

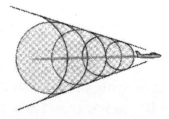

Yeager controlled the X-1's speed by igniting between one and four of his rocket engines. By the time all four engines were lit, he had reached 14,000m (45,000ft). The sky turned from bright blue to dark indigo. Yeager was on the edge of space and flying close to the speed of sound at Mach 0.8.

Down at Muroc, the research engineers and airbase technicians not working on the X-1 showed little interest in the project. In fact, they all thought it was doomed to failure and tragedy. Experienced test pilots had been warned off volunteering for the flights. Most people thought Goodlin had got out just in time.

But up on the roof of the sky, the X-1 was flying beautifully. Yeager had reached maximum speed for this flight and still had half his fuel left. He thought it was time to show the Muroc personnel what his plane could do, so he cut the engines and dived toward the airbase. Lining up the rocket with the main runway he took it down to 90m (300ft) and headed for the control tower. Then Yeager hit the rocket ignition switches.

The four engines burst into life with an enormous streak of flame, making a roar that rattled every roof, window and coffee cup in the base. The X-1 shot back into the sky so fast it reached 11,000m (35,000ft) in under a minute. The fuel cut out, and

Yeager glided down to the main runway, so excited he could not speak.

Yeager might have been pleased with himself, but everyone else was furious. His commanding officer Colonel Boyd told him angrily that the X-1 project was one of the most dangerous test-flights ever attempted. There was no space for fooling around.

The next few trips were extremely dangerous. On its sixth powered flight on October 5, the X-1 started to buffet violently as Yeager reached Mach 0.86. Through the window he could see the rocket's wings shaking wildly as shock waves assaulted his craft.

The next flight was even worse. As Yeager pushed the X-1 to Mach 0.94 he found the control wheel jammed. This was serious. At the speed of sound it was assumed that the aircraft nose would either point up or down – something that the pilot would have to correct. If he was unable to do this, the craft could spin out of control and crash.

Yeager returned to base, sure that the X-1 project would be cancelled. Everyone agreed, apart from Jack Ridley, who quickly scribbled some calculations on a piece of scrap paper. The flight engineer explained that the reason the control wheel jammed was that, at such high speed, the force of the air flowing over the rocket prevented the wing and tail elevators from moving. Instead, suggested Ridley, the aircraft could be controlled by moving the stabilizers on the tail, where the force of the air was not so strong. Yeager had not done this before, because he was afraid the tail might rip off, plunging the plane into an uncontrollable spin which would end with his death in a fiery explosion.

There was only one way to test Ridley's theory. Yeager flew back up to Mach 0.94, a whisker away from the speed of sound. Sure enough, Ridley was right. Moving the stabilizer controls was enough to keep the X-1 flying steady, and gave Yeager the confidence to know that he would be able to keep control of his aircraft.

Yeager now felt sure that he could break the sound barrier in the X-1 and survive. The next X-1 test flight was planned for the following Tuesday – October 14, 1947.

On Sunday evening, Yeager took his wife Glennis out riding, but disaster struck when he was thrown from his horse and fractured two ribs. The pain was intense but Yeager refused to go to the hospital at Muroc. He knew they would stop him from flying and he was determined to finish the job he had started.

So, on the Monday morning before the flight, Glennis drove him to a local doctor who patched him up and told him to rest. But rest was the last thing on his mind. Despite the fact that he could do very little with his right hand, Yeager drove over to Muroc and confided in Jack Ridley. He was convinced he could still make Tuesday's flight. He knew the aircraft really well now, and most of the controls would be no problem to operate.

However, lifting the handle to lock the door of the X-1 required more strength than his painful right arm could muster. In the cramped cockpit he could not reach it with his left hand. But he managed to think of a solution. Ridley found a broom and sawed off 25cm (10in). Yeager could use his good left arm to push the handle up with it. Getting down the ladder would be difficult too, and Yeager jokingly suggested that Ridley could carry him piggyback.

The B-29 took off at 8:00 in the morning that Tuesday. Officially, Yeager was only meant to go to Mach 0.97. But he reasoned that the more flights there were, the more chance there was of an accident. He could be killed or the project could be cancelled. He was going to go for bust.

Getting down the ladder with two broken ribs hurt terribly, but the broomstick worked well on the door handle. As the X-1 dropped from the bomb bay, Yeager felt perfectly in control. He ignited the rocket engines in quick succession and streaked towards the top of the sky. At Mach 0.88, the buffeting started, and Yeager cut two of his engines and tilted the tail stabilizers. They worked perfectly too, and the X-1 stopped shaking. He kicked in rocket engine three and continued to climb. The faster he went, the smoother the ride. The needle in his Mach instrument began to flutter, and then wavered off the scale.

Aircraft flying faster than sound create air turbulence which causes an explosive noise called a "sonic boom." Down at Muroc, a sound like distant thunder rolled over the airfield.

Yeager was elated. He radioed Jack Ridley in the B-29.

"Hey Ridley," he giggled, "that Machmeter is acting screwy. It just went off the scale on me."

"Son, I think you must be imagining things," Ridley responded.

"Must be," said Yeager in his particularly slow drawl. "I'm still wearing my ears and nothing else fell off, neither."

Only his instruments told Yeager he had broken the sound barrier. The X-1 was streaking smoothly along and, as he was flying faster than sound, he did not even hear the sonic boom.

When its fuel ran out, the rocket coasted down to Earth. Yeager landed seven minutes later, to a hero's welcome. His ribs ached terribly, but the desert sun felt wonderful on his face. Not since Orville and Wilbur Wright made the first powered flight in 1903 had an aircraft made such an extraordinary journey.

Afterwards

Yeager's pioneering flight paved the way for all subsequent supersonic jet plane development. Following his record-breaking journey, he spent another decade working as a test pilot.

In the 1960s, Yeager returned to active service, flying bombing missions over Vietnam. He rose to the rank of Brigadier General. Over his life he has logged more than 10,000 hours of flying time, in over 180 different military aircraft. "The best pilots fly more than others," he once said. "That's why they're the best."

His assault on the sound barrier was captured spectacularly in the 1983 American film *The Right*

Stuff, starring Sam Shepard. Based on Tom Wolfe's best-selling book of the same title, the film also depicts America's first attempts to launch an astronaut into space. Yeager worked as a technical advisor on the film, and also made a brief cameo appearance as a bartender at an inn near Muroc airbase.

In retirement, Yeager spends his life hunting, flying (anything from hang-gliders to high speed jets) and making regular appearances as an after-dinner speaker. "I'm not the rocking-chair type," he remarked in his 1986 autobiography *Yeager*.

Animal heroes

The following four short stories show how some people owe their lives or freedom to acts of animal heroism.

Jan's best friend

There are many stories about dogs who have saved their owner's lives by pulling them from swollen rivers, or alerting them to house fires or gas leaks. But few people can have had such a loyal companion, nor owed so much to their dog, as Jan Bozdech of Czechoslovakia.

A few years before the Second World War, Bozdech came across a starving German Shepherd puppy who had been abandoned. He adopted the dog, named it Antis, and the two became inseparable.

When the German army occupied his country in 1938, Bozdech fled to France, taking Antis with him. When war broke out he volunteered to become a pilot in the French Air Force and flew several missions, taking his faithful companion with him in his fighter plane. The two were shot down but survived. When France was also conquered by the Germans, pilot and dog left for England, where Bozdech joined the British Air Force.

When the war ended in 1945, they returned home. But Bozdech's troubles were far from over. Czechoslovakia was now controlled by the Soviet Union rather than Nazi Germany. Shortly after he returned, a strict communist system was set up in his country, and citizens were forbidden to leave.

Bozdech had spent most of the last decade fighting such tyranny and was determined to escape. With Antis and two friends he set off for Austria, the nearest non-communist country. His friends were not happy to travel with the dog, but Antis soon proved his worth, alerting them whenever they were close to police or border guard patrols by growling or looking wary.

Along the way, the escapers had to cross a fast-flowing river under cover of darkness. During the crossing Bozdech slipped, bashed his head on a boulder, and was carried away unconscious by the current. Antis bounded after him, grabbed Bozdech's jacket in his teeth, and dragged him to the riverside. As he lay recovering, the German Shepherd trotted off to find his two friends who had vanished into the night.

Near the border, the party stopped to rest in a quiet spot, leaving the dog to keep watch. After a while, a border guard appeared and began to walk directly toward the sleeping men. Antis immediately started to bark and leaped around the guard, distracting him from his route and saving the three escapers from almost certain arrest.

Once they had safely reached Austria, Bozdech and Antis were able to make their way back to England, where Bozdech had many friends. Antis died in 1953 and Bozdech had him buried at Ilford Animal Cemetery in London. His grave is still there today, and you can see these words written on his gravestone:

There is an old belief
That on some solemn shore
Beyond the sphere of grief
Dear friends shall meet once more.

Goose saves guardsman's bacon

Coldstream guardsman Jack Kemp stood to attention on guard duty at a farm outside Quebec. The year was 1837 and Kemp's regiment had been sent to Canada by the British government to defend the territory from French settlers, who were rebelling against British rule.

As Kemp surveyed the countryside before him, he noticed a handsome white goose searching for food. Close by, and watching intently, was a hungry fox. Sensing danger, the goose looked up. Both animals stood frozen, as if in a trance. Then the goose panicked, and ran shrieking between the guardsman's legs. Kemp reacted instinctively, and when the fox came hurtling after, he killed it with his bayonet.

Much to Kemp's surprise, the goose started to rub his head affectionately against his legs, as if to say thank you. From that moment on, the guardsman adopted him as a pet and gave him the name of Jacob. It was an alliance that was to save his life.

Shortly afterwards, Kemp was standing guard again outside the farm when he was attacked by a group of French rebels. As he fought for his life Jacob came squawking to the rescue, flapping his wings wildly and pecking with his sharp beak. While the distracted rebels defended themselves from the angry goose, Kemp grabbed a rifle that had been knocked from his hand and fired. The shot alerted soldiers nearby who came to his rescue and the attackers ran off. Jacob had saved both Kemp and his comrades. The guardsmen gave Jacob a gold collar as a reward for his bravery. They became so attached to their unusual pet that they took him with them when the regiment returned to London.

The snow dog

New Jersey winters can be harsh. When a blizzard strikes, children are sometimes unable to travel to school, as roads become blocked and driving is impossible. On a day like this in February, 1983, Andrea Andersen and her sisters were stuck at their seaside home. Andrea soon became bored and suggested to her sisters that they go outside to play. Putting on their warmest clothes, they walked through a howling gale to the sea front, but the sisters soon returned home, complaining that it was too cold to be out. Andrea, though, was determined to stay longer.

Alone now, Andrea snuggled deep into her coat and watched the snow tumble down over the choppy waters of the North Atlantic. Suddenly, a strong gust of wind picked her up and blew her into a snowdrift, right on the edge of the icy sea. Andrea was so numb with cold she could hardly move, and became increasingly terrified to discover she did not have the strength to pull herself out. She shouted frantically for help at the top of her voice, but her cries were swallowed by the wind.

But help was at hand. Next door to the Andersen's lived a couple named Dick and Lynda Veit, who kept a Newfoundland dog named Villa. Dogs have much more sensitive hearing than humans, and Villa was able to recognize Andrea's desperate cries above the noise of the raging storm. Immediately, the dog left the house, leaped over a 1.5m (5ft) wall, and set off to look for the girl.

After a brief search among the snow, Villa found Andrea and lowered its big head into the drift. Andrea, who was feeling colder and weaker by the minute, could not believe her luck. She reached up and fastened her freezing fingers around Villa's collar. The Newfoundland pulled her out, and then led the helpless schoolgirl back to the warmth and safety of her home.

When news of the incident broke, Villa was awarded a "Ken-L Ration" medal, for "outstanding loyalty and intelligence", by the Quaker Oats Company, that produces Ken-L dog food. The medal came with a year's supply of dog food.

Heroic homing pigeons

Pigeons have the ability to fly over great distances and return to one particular spot which they think of as home. Soldiers have long made use of this phenomenon by employing these birds to ferry messages, which are carried in a metal tube on the pigeon's leg. Birds used to do this are called homing pigeons, or carrier pigeons.

Some pigeons give up easily in difficult circumstances, but others are determined to return. Pigeons have completed their missions with bullet wounds, or after being mauled by a hawk. One even walked back home with a broken wing.

During the First and Second World Wars, carrier pigeons were used in great numbers and many men owed their lives to the birds. In Italy in 1943, one American carrier pigeon named G.I. Joe flew 32km (20 miles) in only 20 minutes, with a message warning a bomber squadron not to attack a village that had just been captured by American troops.

Another pigeon named Winkie was aboard a British bomber when it crashed in the North Sea. The crew survived but, as no one at their base knew their position, they were in danger of freezing to death. Winkie was covered in oil but this did not prevent him from flying the long journey home, with a message reporting that the plane had crashed in the sea, and a detailed map reference showing where the crew could be found. Thanks to Winkie's perserverance, a search was immediately launched and the crew's lives were saved.

Stauffenberg's Secret Germany

On a spring morning in 1943, American fighter planes screamed low over a Tunisian coastal road, pouring machine-gun fire onto a column of German army vehicles. Fierce flames bellowed from blazing trucks and smeared the blue desert sky with oily, black smoke. Amid the wreckage on the ground lay Colonel Claus von Stauffenberg, one of Germany's most brilliant soldiers. He was badly wounded, and fighting for his life.

Stauffenberg was quickly transported to a Munich hospital and given the best possible treatment. His left eye, right hand and two fingers from his left hand had been lost in the attack. His legs were so badly damaged that doctors feared he would never walk again.

Willing himself back from the brink of death, Stauffenberg was determined not to be defeated by his injuries. He refused all pain-killing drugs, and learned to dress, bathe and write with his three remaining fingers. His recovery was astounding.

Before the summer was over he was demanding to be returned to his regiment.

Hospital staff were amazed by their patient's stubborn persistence, and admired what they thought was his patriotic determination to return to active service. But it was not to fight for Nazi leader Adolf Hitler that the colonel struggled so hard to recover. What Stauffenberg wanted to do was kill him.

Stauffenberg had supported the Nazis once, but his experience in the war had turned him against them. In Poland, in 1939, he had witnessed SS soldiers killing Jewish women and children by the roadside. While fighting in France in 1940, he had seen a Nazi field commander order the execution of unarmed British prisoners. Worst of all had been Hitler's war against the Soviet Union (now Russia). Not only had this invasion been fought with great brutality to Russian soldiers and civilians alike, but Stauffenberg had been sickened by Hitler's incompetent interference in the campaign, and his stubborn refusal to allow exhausted troops in impossible situations to surrender.

After one disastrous battle, Stauffenberg asked a close friend: "Is there no officer in Hitler's headquarters capable of taking a pistol to the beast?" Lying in his hospital bed, Stauffenberg realized he was just the man for the job.

Like most people, Stauffenberg had his flaws. Although he was untidy in his personal appearance, he was incredibly strict about orderliness and punctuality. He had a ferocious temper, and could become enraged if an aide laid out his uniform less than perfectly. But Stauffenberg was blessed with a magnetic personality and he was a brilliant commander. He also had a sensitive nature, which encouraged fellow officers to confide in him. All these aspects of his character made him an ideal leader of any opposition to Hitler.

As soon as Stauffenberg was well enough to come out of hospital, he was appointed Chief of Staff in the Home Army. The Home Army was a unit of the German Army made up of all soldiers stationed in Germany. It was also responsible for recruitment and training. Stauffenberg quickly established that the deputy commander of the Home Army, General Olbricht, was not a supporter of the Nazis either. He too was willing to help Stauffenberg overthrow Hitler. Between them, they began to persuade other officers to join them.

Stauffenberg and his fellow plotters soon devised an ingenious plan to get rid of Hitler. In the previous year, the Nazis had set up a strategy called *Operation*

Valkyrie, as a precaution against an uprising in Germany against them. If such a revolt broke out, the Home Army had detailed instructions to seize control of all areas of government, and important radio and railway stations, so the rebellion could be quickly put down.

But, rather than protect the Nazis, Stauffenberg and Olbricht intended to use *Operation Valkyrie* to overthrow them. They planned to kill Hitler and, in the confusion that followed his death, they would set *Operation Valkyrie* in motion, ordering their soldiers to arrest all Nazi leaders and their chief supporters – especially the SS (elite regiments of Nazi soldiers) and the Gestapo (secret police).

The plot had two great flaws. Firstly, killing Hitler would be difficult, as he was surrounded by bodyguards. Secondly, when the head of the Home Army, General Friedrich Fromm, was approached by the conspirators, he refused to take part. Like everyone in the armed forces, he had sworn an oath of loyalty to Hitler, and he used this as an excuse for not betraying him. Fromm also feared Hitler's revenge if the plot should fail. Without Fromm's help, using Valkyrie to overthrow the Nazis would be considerably more difficult.

But the plotters were not deterred and Stauffenberg still threw himself into the task of recruiting allies. He referred to his conspiracy as "Secret Germany" after a poem by his hero, German writer Stefan George. Many officers joined Stauffenberg, but many more wavered. Most were disgusted by the way Hitler was leading the German army but, like Fromm, they felt restrained by their oath of loyalty or feared for their lives if the plot should fail.

The plotters took care to avoid being discovered by the Gestapo. Documents were typed wearing gloves, to avoid leaving fingerprints, on a typewriter that would then be hidden in a cupboard or attic. Stauffenberg memorized and then destroyed written messages, and left not a scrap of solid evidence against himself. And such was his good judgment in recruiting plotters that not a single German officer he approached to join the conspiracy betrayed him.

But by the summer of 1944, time was running out. The Gestapo had begun to suspect a major revolt against Hitler was being planned. They were searching hard for conspirators and the evidence to condemn them. The longer the plotters delayed, the greater their chance of being discovered.

By this time, the plotters had decided the best way to kill Hitler would be with a bomb hidden in a briefcase. As part of his Home Army duties, Stauffenberg attended conferences with the German leader, who thought the colonel was a very glamorous figure and had a high regard for his abilities. Because Stauffenberg had such close personal contact with Hitler, he volunteered to plant the bomb himself.

In order to give him time to escape, the bomb would be primed with a ten-minute fuse. This device was quite complicated. To activate the bomb, a small glass tube containing acid needed to be broken with a pair of pliers. The acid would eat through a thin steel wire. When this broke, it released a detonator which set off the bomb.

On July 11, Stauffenberg went to Hitler's headquarters at Rastenburg in East Prussia for a meeting with Hitler, and two other leading Nazis, Heinrich Himmler and Herman Goring. He hoped to wipe out all three, but when Himmler and Goring did not arrive he decided to wait for a better opportunity.

On July 15, Stauffenberg was again summoned to Rastenburg. On this occasion, *Operation Valkyrie* was set in motion before the meeting. But unfortunately, at the last moment, Hitler decided not to attend the conference where Stauffenberg was due to plant his bomb. A frantic phone call to Berlin called off *Valkyrie* and the conspirators covered their tracks by pretending it had been an army exercise.

Their chance finally came on July 20, 1944, when Stauffenberg was again summoned to Hitler's headquarters at Rastenburg. Together with his personal assistant, Lieutenant Werner von Haeften, he collected two bombs and drove to Rangsdorf airfield south of Berlin, and from there took the three hour flight to Rastenburg.

Arriving in East Prussia at 10:15am, they drove through gloomy forest to Hitler's headquarters. Surrounded by barbed wire, minefields and checkpoints, the base – fancifully known as "The Wolf's Lair"– was a collection of concrete bunkers and wooden huts. It was here, cut off from the real world, that Hitler had retreated to wage his final battles of the war.

The conference with Hitler was scheduled for 12:30pm. At 12:15pm, as conference staff began to assemble, Stauffenberg requested permission to wash and change his shirt. It was such a hot day this seemed perfectly reasonable.

An aide ushered him into a nearby washroom, where he was quickly joined by Haeften, and they set about activating the two bombs. Stauffenberg broke the acid tube fuse on one but, as he reached for the second bomb, they were interrupted by a sergeant sent to hurry Stauffenberg, who was now late for the conference.

One bomb would have to do. But there was further bad news. Stauffenberg had hoped the meeting would be held in an underground bunker – a windowless, concrete room where the blast of his bomb would be much more destructive. But instead, he was led to a wooden hut with three large windows. The force of any explosion here would be a lot less effective.

Inside the hut, the conference had already begun. High-ranking officers and their assistants crowded around a large, oak, map table, discussing the progress of the war in Russia. Stauffenberg, whose hearing had been damaged when he was wounded, asked if he could stand near to Hitler so he could hear him properly.

Placing himself to Hitler's right, Stauffenberg shoved his bulging briefcase under the table, to the left of a large, wooden support. Just then, Field Marshal Keitel, who was one of Hitler's most loyal generals, suggested that Stauffenberg should deliver his report next. But with less than seven minutes before the bomb would explode, he had no intention of remaining inside the hut. Fortunately, the discussion on the Russian front continued and Stauffenberg made an excuse to leave the room, saying he had to make an urgent phone call to Berlin.

Keitel, already irritated by Stauffenberg's late arrival, became incensed that he should have the impertinence to leave the conference, and called after him, insisting that he should stay. But Stauffenberg ignored him and hurried off. Like all the conspirators, he hated Keitel, whom he called Lakeitel – a pun on the German word *Lakei* meaning "toady" or "lackey."

There were less than five minutes to go. Stauffenberg hurried over to another hut and waited with his friend General Erich Fellgiebel, the chief of signals at the base, who was one of several Rastenburg officers who had joined Stauffenberg's conspiracy. The seconds dragged by.

Inside the conference room, an officer named Colonel Brandt leaned over the table to get a better look at a map. As he did so, his foot caught on Stauffenberg's heavy briefcase, so he picked it up and moved it to the opposite side of the heavy, wooden support. An instant later, at 12:42pm precisely, the bomb went off.

The Wolf's Lair Conference Room

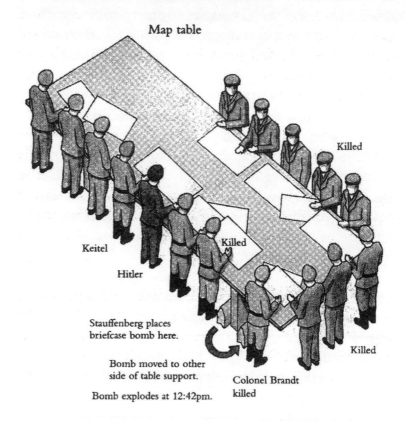

Map table

Killed

Killed

Keitel

Hitler

Killed

Stauffenberg places
briefcase bomb here.

Bomb moved to other
side of table support.

Colonel Brandt
killed

Bomb explodes at 12:42pm.

At the sound of the explosion, Haeften drove up
in a staff car and Stauffenberg leapt in. The two of
them had to escape to the airfield quickly, before
"The Wolf's Lair" was sealed off by Hitler's guards.
The hut looked completely devastated and, as they
drove away, both felt confident no one inside could
have survived.

They were wrong. Brandt and three others had been killed but, in moving the briefcase to the other side of the wooden support, Brandt had shielded Hitler from the full force of the blast. The German leader staggered out of the hut, his hair smoldering and trousers in tatters. He was very much alive.

Fellgiebel watched in horror. Hitler's death was an essential part of the plot. But, nonetheless, shortly before 1:00pm he sent a message to the War Office in Berlin, confirming the bomb had exploded and ordering Olbricht to set *Valkyrie* into operation. He made no mention of whether Hitler was alive or dead.

But back in Berlin, Olbricht hesitated because he was uncertain whether Hitler was dead. Until he knew more, he was not prepared to act. Meanwhile Stauffenberg, flying back to Berlin, was cut off from everything. During the two hours he was in the air, he expected his fellow conspirators to be carrying through *Operation Valkyrie* in a frenzy of activity. In fact, nothing was happening. Unfortunately for the plotters, Stauffenberg could not be in two places at once. He was the best man to carry out the bomb attack in Rastenburg, but he would also have been the best man to direct *Operation Valkyrie* in Berlin.

At Rastenburg, it did not take long to realize who had planted the bomb. Orders were immediately issued to arrest Stauffenberg at Berlin's Rangsdorf airfield. But the signals officer responsible for sending this message was also one of the conspirators, and the order was never transmitted.

Only after an hour and a half, at 3:30pm, did the Berlin conspirators reluctantly begin to act. Home Army officers were summoned by Olbricht and told that Hitler was dead and *Operation Valkyrie* was to be set in motion. But General Fromm was still refusing to cooperate, especially after he phoned Rastenburg and was told by General Keitel that Hitler was alive.

At 4:30pm, the plotters grew bolder and issued orders to the entire German army. Hitler, they declared, was dead. Nazi party leaders were trying to seize power for themselves. The army was to take control of the government immediately, to stop them from doing this.

Stauffenberg arrived back in Berlin soon afterwards. He too was not able to persuade Fromm to join the conspiracy. Instead the commander-in-chief erupted into a foaming tirade against him. Banging his fists on his desk, Fromm demanded that the conspirators be placed under arrest and ordered Stauffenberg to shoot himself. When Fromm began to lunge at his fellow officers, fists flailing, he had to be subdued with a pistol pressed to his stomach. Then he meekly allowed himself to be locked in an office. Other officers at Home Army headquarters who were still loyal to the Nazis were also locked up.

Stauffenberg's final day

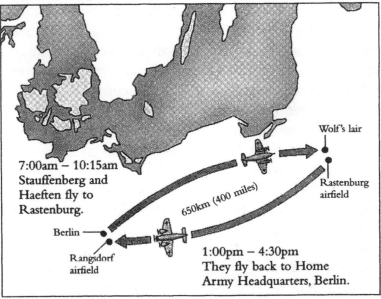

7:00am – 10:15am Stauffenberg and Haeften fly to Rastenburg.

Wolf's lair

Rastenburg airfield

650km (400 miles)

Berlin

Rangsdorf airfield

1:00pm – 4:30pm They fly back to Home Army Headquarters, Berlin.

Stauffenberg now began to direct the conspirators with his usual energy and verve. For the rest of the afternoon, they worked with desperate haste to carry out their plan. Stauffenberg spent hours on the phone trying to persuade reluctant or wavering army commanders to support him. He was still convinced Hitler was dead, but many of the people he spoke to would not believe him. At the time, it was widely believed that the Nazi leader employed a double who looked and acted just like him. What if Stauffenberg had killed the double rather than the real Hitler, they thought.

From Paris to Prague, the army attempted to take control and arrest all Nazi officials. In some cities such as Vienna and Paris there were remarkable successes, but in Berlin it was another story. Here, the plotters were foiled by their own decency. They had revolted against the brutality of the Nazi regime and, ironically, only a similar ruthlessness could have saved them. If the conspirators had been prepared to shoot anyone who stood in their way, they might have succeeded.

They failed to capture Berlin's radio station and army communication bases in the capital. All through the late afternoon, their own commands were constantly contradicted by orders transmitted by commanders loyal to the Nazis.

By early evening it became obvious to Stauffenberg that the plot had failed yet, true to his character, he refused to give up. He insisted that success was just a whisker away and he continued to encourage his fellow plotters not to give up hope. But the end was near.

The War Office was now surrounded by hostile troops loyal to Hitler and, inside the building, a small group of Nazi officers had armed themselves and set out to arrest the conspirators. Shots were fired, Stauffenberg was hit in the shoulder and Fromm was released.

Fromm could only do one thing. Although he had refused to cooperate with the plotters, he had known all about the plot. No doubt the conspirators would confirm this – under torture or of their own free will. Fromm had to cover his tracks. He sentenced Stauffenberg, Haeften, Olbricht and his assistant Colonel Mertz von Quirnheim to immediate execution.

Stauffenberg was bleeding badly from his wound, but seemed indifferent to his death sentence. He insisted the plot was all his doing. His fellow officers had simply been carrying out his orders.

Fromm was having none of this. Just after midnight, the four men were hustled down the stairs to the courtyard outside. By all accounts, they went calmly to their deaths. Lit by the dimmed headlights of a staff car, the four were shot in order of rank. Stauffenberg was second, after Olbricht. An instant before the firing squad cut Stauffenberg down, Haeften, in a brave but pointless gesture, threw himself in front of the bullets. Stauffenberg died moments later, shouting: "Long live our Secret Germany."

There would have been more executions that night, had not Gestapo chief Kaltenbrunner arrived and put a stop to them. He was far more interested in seeing what could be learned from the conspirators who were still alive.

Still, the Gestapo torturers had been cheated of their greatest prize. Stauffenberg and his fellow martyrs were buried that night in a nearby churchyard. They had failed, but their bravery in the face of such a slim chance of success had been truly heroic.

Afterwards

If Stauffenberg and his conspirators had succeeded with *Operation Valkyrie*, the war in Europe might have ended much earlier. As it was, it continued for almost another year. In those final months of the Second World War, more people were killed than in the previous five years of fighting.

Hitler described the conspiracy as "a crime unparalleled in German history" and reacted accordingly. Although Stauffenberg, von Haeften, Olbricht and Mertz were dead and buried, Hitler demanded that their bodies be dug up, burned, and the ashes scattered to the wind.

Following brutal interrogation, the main surviving conspirators were hauled before the Nazi courts. They refused to be intimidated, knowing the regime they loathed was teetering on the brink of defeat. General Erich Fellgiebel, who had stood with Stauffenberg as the bomb exploded at Rastenburg, was told by the court president that he was to be hanged. "Hurry with the hanging Mr. President," he replied, "otherwise you will hang earlier than we."

Gestapo and SS officers investigated the plot until the last days of the war. Seven thousand arrests were made, and between two and three thousand people were executed. Among·them was General Fromm. Although he had never joined the conspirators, he was shot for cowardice in failing to prevent them from carrying out their revolt.

Stauffenberg's personal magnetism continued to exert an extraordinary influence, even from beyond the grave. SS investigator Georg Kiesel was so in awe of him, he reported to Hitler that his assassin was "a spirit of fire, fascinating and inspiring all who came in touch with him."

Alexei Stakhanov – Soviet superstar

During the First World War, the Russian Empire collapsed into chaos and, in 1917, a revolution swept away the old regime. Russia's new rulers renamed their country the Soviet Union. They set up a communist society where citizens were supposed to have equality, and the state took control of all the country's farms and industry.

A decade later Russia was still very poor. Dictator Joseph Stalin, who ruled his people with an iron grip, was determined to transform his country into a powerful nation ready to defend itself from enemies.

In 1931 he broadcast a speech to the whole Soviet Union, saying: "We are 50 or 100 years behind the advanced countries," meaning the capitalist nations of Europe, the United States, Japan and others. "We must make good this distance in ten years. Either we do it, or they crush us."

He gave orders for huge factories, steel works and coal mines to be built. In Stalin's plan, workers on these projects, fired with enthusiasm for their new communist nation, would go on to produce record levels of materials.

But most workers in these new plants and factories were peasants. In the 1920s and 30s, 17 million of them moved from villages and farm work to towns and industry. Packed into unfamiliar cities, away from their close-knit country communities, many felt disoriented and unsettled. New to the routine of factory jobs, they were ill-disciplined and apathetic.

Execution or imprisonment was Stalin's usual method of persuading people to do what he wanted, but for this situation he had another tactic. If other countries made heroes of film stars or royalty, then the Soviet Union would have heroes of industry. His henchmen were dispatched to find a suitable candidate.

On September 1, 1935, Soviet citizens woke to read in their morning papers that coal miner Alexei Stakhanov had dug out an extraordinary amount of coal in a Donbass mine during the night shift of August 30-31. It was fourteen times the amount a miner was expected to produce in a single shift. The papers talked of his efforts in heroic, military terms. He was a "shock worker" who had made a "breakthrough" on the "coal production front." The message was clear, the papers said. If an ordinary miner could perform such superhuman work, then "there are no fortresses communism cannot storm."

In a carefully set-up media campaign, Stakhanov was overwhelmed with attention. He spoke on the radio, starred in newsreels, appeared in propaganda posters and was awarded the Order of Lenin, the Soviet Union's most prestigious medal. He moved to Moscow where he became the figurehead for the so-called "Stakhanovite" movement, which encouraged other workers to follow his example.

How could one man do the work of 14? Stakhanov told the Soviet people he had been inspired by a speech of Stalin's, which he had heard on the radio the evening of his heroic shift. The truth was that his feat was a confidence trick set up by the Soviet authorities. Two other miners had actually helped him dig the coal. Then a team of workers had carried it from the coalface, and done a range of other jobs a miner would usually have to do for himself on an ordinary shift.

The truth was that Stakhanov was not even an exceptional worker. He had been selected for hero status because his handsome face would look good in photographs and, equally important, because he was a docile, easy-going fellow, unlikely to question what he was being asked to do.

The "Stakhanovite" movement created other heroes, from steel workers to milkmaids whose cows produced record levels of milk. ("Storm the 3,000 litre level" ran one slogan.) They starred in newsreels and were celebrated in biographies. "Stakhanovites" were rewarded with extra pay or prestigious apartments. But many were unpopular with their fellow workers, who felt their exceptional workmate showed up the rest of them in a bad light. Some "Stakhanovites" were attacked or even murdered.

And what of Stakhanov himself? The Soviet superman who exchanged the Donbass coal fields for a desk in Moscow proved to be a poor organizer. When other workplace heroes sprang up to replace him, he was quietly dropped from his post, and vanished into obscurity.

Afterwards

Stalin's attempt to build a powerful industrial nation succeeded just in time. The Soviet Union was invaded by Nazi Germany in 1941. The Nazis nearly overran the country but the Soviet army, fighting with great heroism and determination, drove them off. However, the army could never have defeated the Nazis without the guns, tanks and aircraft built in Stalin's new factories.

Stakhanov enjoyed his moment of fame, but adjusted badly to life away from the spotlight. He turned to drink, and died a bitter man in 1977. Despite the obscurity of his later years, he still featured prominently in Soviet school history books and it was only in 1988 that the Soviet people were finally told that his legendary record was a sham.

Blackbeard meets his match

The years between 1690 and 1730 were the "Golden Age of Piracy". Cargo ships sailing from Europe to North and South America and Africa were regularly plundered by gangs of pirates, most of which were British.

These pirates were much feared by the sailors they preyed upon, none more so than Edward "Blackbeard" Teach. A whole head taller than most and built like a bear, Teach's nickname came from his huge, black beard. Stretching down to his chest, it was usually braided with bright ribbons, and covered a face that was in constant contact with a bottle of rum.

Originally a slave trader from Bristol, England, Teach did have a certain roguish charm. But the string of women who married him (14 in all) usually came to regret their decision – especially when he insisted on sharing them with the rest of his crew. He was certainly never dull company. Once, during a lull in plundering, he suggested to his crew that they create tortures of their own, to see who could last the longest. He and three shipmates had themselves sealed into the ship's hold with several pots of blazing, foul-smelling gas. Naturally, Teach won, and emerged on the deck to announce they ought to have a hanging contest – to see who could last the longest dangling from a noose.

It was all good training for his crew's likely prospects. "A merry life and a short one shall be my motto" wrote another pirate captain, Bartholomew Roberts. The risks of piracy, after all, were great – death in battle or public execution. Yet the rewards were extraordinary. A successful pirate, who in everyday life might struggle to earn a pittance as a sailor, mill worker or miner, could make as much in a year as a wealthy aristocrat.

Teach was not all fun and games. He usually went into battle with several slow-burning fuses woven into his hair. With his already terrifying features cloaked in a haze of smoke, he looked like a demon from his lair and frightened his opponents witless.

Captured crews who had put up a fight could expect no mercy. Teach even cut off the nose of one Portuguese captive and made him eat it. His own companions sometimes fared no better – he was reputed to have killed one of his crew just to remind them how evil he was.

This was all above and beyond the needs of ordinary piracy, but it served a purpose. As his reputation spread, few of the merchant ships he attacked dared to oppose him. Hoping to make as much profit as possible, greedy traders manned their ships with small, badly paid and badly armed crews. Faced with a horde of ruthless pirates, many were not willing to defend their cargoes with their lives.

Teach's hunting grounds were the coastal waters of North America. Here his plundered wealth brought him friends in high places, who alerted him to the whereabouts of Navy ships or soldiers, and allowed him to trade his stolen goods in coastal settlements. But by 1715, his activities – and those of other pirates in the Caribbean and Atlantic coast of America – were having such a bad effect on trade that he could no longer be ignored. Cargo ships had to travel with naval escorts, and the cost of insuring their goods became so expensive it was hardly worth transporting them. Something had to be done, but who could be found to fight such a formidable foe?

Alexander Spotswood, Governor of Virginia, put up a reward of £100 (then nearly 10 years wages for an ordinary seaman), hoping to attract someone whose lust for wealth or glory outweighed his fear of this most evil of pirates. As well as advertising this reward, he also called in the Royal Navy, and paid for a search party of two ships from his own personal fortune.

So, on November 17, 1718, Lieutenant Robert Maynard, commander of the Royal Navy warship *HMS Pearl*, set sail from Virginia to look for Teach, together with a smaller ship *HMS Lyme*. Altogether he had 60 men under his command. Maynard had been told that Teach had based himself in Ocracoke Inlet, North Carolina, and his small search party arrived there just before dusk four days later.

Maynard soon spotted Teach's ship, the *Adventurer*, and dropped his anchor some distance away. He planned to attack the next morning. That night the pirates had a party, and their drunken curses drifted across the water between the two ships. Maynard's anxious crew wondered what sort of men they would have to fight on the coming day.

Daybreak finally came, and Maynard ordered his attack to begin. It started very badly. Ocracoke Inlet is shallow, and no sooner had Maynard's ships moved against the *Adventurer* than they became stuck in

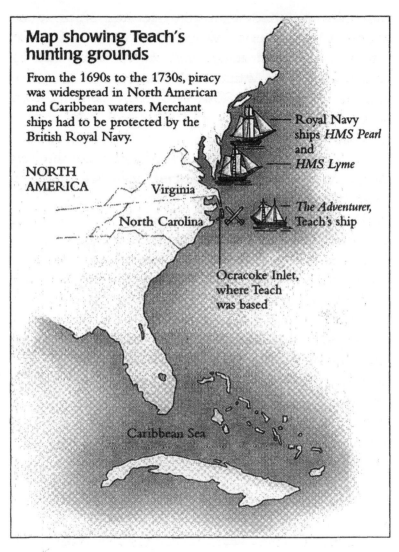

Map showing Teach's hunting grounds

From the 1690s to the 1730s, piracy was widespread in North American and Caribbean waters. Merchant ships had to be protected by the British Royal Navy.

NORTH AMERICA

Virginia

North Carolina

Royal Navy ships *HMS Pearl* and *HMS Lyme*

The Adventurer, Teach's ship

Ocracoke Inlet, where Teach was based

Caribbean Sea

sandbanks. Only when several heavy weights had been thrown out of the vessels were they able to move on.

Teach watched the approaching ships with drunken amusement. When the *Pearl* was close enough, he called across the water, demanding to know what they wanted. Maynard knew all about Teach's reputation, but nevertheless he was determined to inspire his frightened men with a courageous response.

"You may see we are no pirates," he shouted defiantly, and boldly announced he was coming to seize Blackbeard and his crew.

Teach was enraged and bellowed a hair-raising series of curses back at Maynard and his men.

Teach's crew was only 19 strong, but they were all seasoned villains and determined to fight to the death. After all, if they were captured alive, they would only be hung as pirates. As the *Adventurer* moved closer to the Navy ships it swung around and fired its cannons. *HMS Lyme* caught the full force of this broadside. Its captain and several of his crew were killed and the ship floundered helplessly in the water. Maynard and the *Pearl* pressed on to face the *Adventurer* alone.

Worse was to come. Blackbeard's next volley hit the *Pearl* with similar force. So intense was the fire that 21 men were injured and Maynard had to order his crew to take cover below. Teach's ship came alongside the deserted deck of the *Pearl* and his pirate crew tossed aboard blazing bottles stuffed full with a mixture of gunpowder, buckshot and scrap iron.

Smoke shrouded the deck of the shattered *Pearl*, and Teach was confident that he had already won an easy victory. His pirates swarmed aboard to take possession of the ship. But, at that moment, Maynard unleashed a counter-attack, and led those of his crew who could still stand out onto the deck. Bayonets flashed and pistols cracked as the two sides clashed in hand-to-hand fighting.

Battling through the chaos Maynard fought his way toward Teach, and both men fired their pistols at point-blank range. Teach's drinking had blurred his senses, and only Maynard found his target. But the bullet that struck the huge pirate seemed to have no effect on him, and he lunged forward with his cutlass. Maynard raised his own sword to deflect the blow, but to his horror it broke in two. Teach towered over him with a rabid leer and raised his cutlass to cut him dead. But the blow never fell.

One of Pearl's crew, rushing to defend his captain, slashed at the pirate's throat. Yet even this was only a distraction. Spurting fountains of blood, Teach drew another pistol from his belt and aimed again at Maynard. Then a strange, faraway look came into his eyes. He swayed, and toppled over like a fallen oak.

The death of the mighty Blackbeard was the turning point of the struggle, and the rest of the pirates were soon killed or surrendered. Ten of *Pearl*'s men lay dead, and all but one of the seamen had been injured.

After the battle, Teach's head was cut off and hung from the Pearl's bow. But such was his fearsome reputation that his body, which was thrown overboard, was said to have swum several times around the ship in brazen defiance before it sank to the bottom of the sea.

Afterwards

Although his victory over the fearsome Teach marked the virtual end of piracy in North America, Maynard was poorly rewarded. Alive, Blackbeard had a price of £100 on his head. Once he was dead, the government authorities refused to pay up.

Four years of legal wrangling followed, as the navy lieutenant tried to secure a fair reward for his crew. He was eventually given a measly £3 for his trouble, and those who fought with him were given half that amount.

The story of Blackbeard and his final battle with Lieutenant Maynard still continues to entertain and intrigue. Several movies have been made about Blackbeard's life. The most well known is the 1952 American film *Blackbeard the Pirate*. Here, Robert Newton plays the infamous villain, and charges around waving pistols and rolling his eyes with immense enthusiasm. The plot takes great liberties with the known facts. Instead of Lieutenant Maynard, reformed pirate Sir Henry Morgan is hired to rid the high seas of the pirate menace. Morgan still has something of a wicked streak in him and Blackbeard comes to a suitably gruesome end. Buried up to his neck on a sandy beach, he is slowly drowned by the incoming tide.

Owens 4, master race 0

American athlete Jesse Owens was fresh off the ocean liner *Manhattan* on his way to the Berlin Olympics. The year was 1936. As his motor coach rolled south-east towards the German capital, he stared out from the window with increasing amazement. The streets of Germany were like nothing he had ever seen before. The old buildings fascinated him, as they did any American who had grown up in a town or city that had only recently been built. But most striking of all were the swastika flags that seemed to hang from almost every window or shop front. The crooked black cross on a blood-red banner was the symbol of the German Nazi Party. Its ubiquitous presence spoke silently of a country in the total control of its political masters.

The 1936 Olympics were held in troubled times. Italy had just conquered Ethiopia; mass unemployment plagued Europe and America; Brazil was so politically divided it sent two teams to the games (both were disqualified); civil war had broken out in Spain that very summer. Most ominously of all, a regime of alarming brutality had taken control in Germany.

The Nazis believed that the German people were the "master race" – superior human beings who were destined to rule the world. To them, the huge 110,000 capacity Berlin Olympic Stadium was to be a grand stage, where German athletes would assert their claims to racial superiority. The whole occasion was one big advertisement for their regime and its sinister beliefs.

The Nazis had strong views about other races too, especially Jews and Black people. Nazi leaders blamed Jews for every evil that had overtaken their country that century, and Jewish people in Germany were subjected to daily abuse and violence. The Nazi attitude to Black people was less complicated – they simply thought of them as subhuman.

Many people throughout the world were disgusted by the racist attitudes of the Nazis, and felt their country should boycott the Olympics. Aware of this disapproval, the Nazis had softened their extremist policies in the months leading up to the Olympics – for example, racist street graffiti, billboards and political newspaper articles denouncing Jews disappeared. For a while it looked as if the Nazis were softening their policies. Eventually 52 nations agreed to attend the Berlin Olympics.

Owens too had wondered whether he should go to Berlin. But at 22 he was one of America's most promising athletes. He was a phenomenal runner and long jumper – in May 1935, at an athletics meeting in Michigan, USA, he had broken three world records in one amazing hour. The Olympic Games offered him the opportunity to show his skills to the entire world.

His coach had warned him to expect racist abuse from Nazi supporters among the Berlin crowds. But Owens had come to the Olympics determined not to allow this to affect his performance. But their expectations were wrong. The German people were fascinated by Owens, and no sooner had he arrived in the country than he was mobbed by sports fans who had read about his record-breaking performances.

Owens made an ideal hero. Being tall and handsome obviously helped, but the athlete had a boyish charm and modesty that made him particularly likable. As he posed for photographs and signed endless autographs, he talked to the crowd in the few words of German he had taken the trouble to learn. Curiously, his popularity proved to be just as much a problem as the hostility he had expected. At night, Owens was kept awake by fans who came to his bedroom window to take photographs or demand autographs.

The Games began on August 1 with a massive celebration designed to glorify the Nazi regime as much as it did the Olympics. Then the founder of the modern Games, Pierre de Coubertin, made a speech to the Berlin spectators, saying: "The important thing at the Olympic Games is not to win, but to take part... the most important thing about life is not to conquer, but to struggle well." It was a philosophy the Nazi hosts of the Games would not be taking seriously.

Owens' first race, the 100m, was on the day after the opening. This brief event is one of the most glamorous and exciting in athletics, and is always the cause of tremendous interest.

Owens felt under enormous pressure in the tense moments before the race he had worked so hard to win. As he arrived at the starting line for the final, he realized that the other five athletes there were the world's fastest human beings. All of them wanted to beat him. Dismissing these thoughts from his head, he focused instead on the finishing line ahead, and reminded himself that the next 10 or so seconds of the race would be the climax of eight years of training.

On that cold, wet afternoon the crowd held its breath, the sound of the starting pistol echoed around the stadium, and Owens shot from the line. He was ahead by the first 10m (30ft). Described by one journalist as having "the grace and poise of a deer", he had a natural style that made running look easy. Sweeping to a new Olympic record and an ecstatic reception from the stadium crowd, he won the race in 10.3 seconds. He would look back on the moment he was presented with his first Olympic gold medal as the happiest of his career.

In his private stadium box, Nazi leader Adolf Hitler, a regular spectator at the Games, was not amused. His dream of German athletes dominating the games was fading before his eyes. When an aide suggested he invite Owens up to congratulate him (as he had with successful German athletes), Hitler was outraged. "Do you really think I will allow myself to be photographed shaking hands with a black man?" he hissed.

The next day Owens competed in the long jump, but his three preliminary jumps nearly ended in disaster. Back home in America, athletes were allowed to make a trial run up to the long jump pit, as a warm-up exercise. Here in Germany, the rules were different. When Owens did this and ran into the sand, the judges indicated that he had failed his first jump. Badly riled, he went on to fail his second jump too.

As he prepared for his vital third jump, help came from an unexpected quarter. A fellow long jump competitor named Lutz Long, who was one of Germany's star athletes, whispered a few consoling words. Encouraged, Owens jumped successfully. The competition ended with Owens jumping to victory against Long in the final. The German just could not match his stupendous, record-breaking 8.06m (over 26ft) leap. "I just decided I wasn't going to come down," Owens later told reporters. The record remained unbeaten for 24 years.

Long and Owens left the stadium arena arm-in-arm, and that evening they met again at the Olympic Village and talked through the night. Long's blond, Germanic good looks and perfectly proportioned athlete's body were the epitome of the Nazi German racial ideal. But Long did not share his leader's racist notions. He and Owens found they had much in common. They were the same age and from similar, poor backgrounds, and both saw athletic success as a passport away from their humble origins. Long too was disturbed by the prejudice he saw all around him in Germany.

There were more successes to come. On August 5, Owens took to the field to run in the 200m final. By now Nazi hopes that their athletes would sweep away all competition had evaporated. The Nazi press had started to ridicule Owens, and German officials were heard complaining about "non-humans" being allowed to take part in the Games.

Owens refused to let himself be intimidated by this atmosphere of petty spite, and won the 200m in a record-breaking 20.7 seconds. He had a particular technique for getting off to a good start. He noticed that the starting official would make some small gesture, a flexing of the legs, or tensing of the facial muscles, just before he fired the starting pistol. From the corner of his eye, Owens would watch for these signs. Forewarned, he would shoot from the starting line the instant the gun fired.

For Owens, the 200m was the final event, and he settled back to enjoy the rest of the Games, free from the pressure of further competition. But the U.S. coaches had other plans for him. He was on such top form they insisted he take part in the 4 x 100m relay.

(Here four athletes run 100m each, passing a baton between them.) It was an unhappy decision, which caused a lot of hard feelings, as the coaches dropped American Jewish athlete Marty Gluckman. Owens himself protested. He'd won three gold medals already, he told the coach, and someone else should be given a chance. The coach was unmoved. "You'll do as you're told," he growled.

So Owens took to the field. The American team was unbeatable. Starting the race, Owens was ahead by several paces by the time he passed the baton on to the second runner. Once again an Olympic record was set by the team, and Owens added a fourth medal to his collection. It was a wonderful end to a wonderful performance, although Owens, with characteristic modesty, insisted another athlete occupy the top spot of the podium during the medals ceremony.

The Berlin Olympics made Owens world-famous. When the games finished he left Germany for a short tour of Europe, surrounded by press photographers and well-wishers. Hitler was deeply irritated by it all. The 1936 Olympic Games were supposed to have been a great victory for the German Master Race. Now no one was going to forget the soft-spoken Black American who had quietly ridiculed Nazi boasts of German racial supremacy.

Afterwards

Back in the Olympic Village, events were taking a more sinister turn. As they left, athletes could hear machine gun fire from nearby fields. The Village was already being turned into an army training camp. Days later, billboards and newspapers in Germany were again filled with anti-Jewish propaganda. The next Olympics were due to take part in 1940. The host nation would be Germany's ally, Japan, but by then, Europe was at war and the Games did not actually take place again until 1948. Hitler fantasized that, following the Nazi conquest of Europe, the Games would be held in Germany forever, and black athletes would be forbidden to compete.

Owens and his Olympic triumph were captured on film by the eminent German director Leni Reifenstahl in *Olympische Spiele 1936*. This sinister but beautiful film is seen by many as a hymn to Germany's Nazi regime, but Reifenstahl made no attempt to play down the victory of Black American Owens over the pride of Germany's athletes.

The long jump record set by Owens remained unbeaten until 1960, but his fame did not bring him happiness. Deluged with showbusiness and business offers, Owens displayed his athletic ability at sideshows and exhibitions, where he would run against racehorses or play with the celebrity basketball team, the Harlem Globetrotters. Badly advised and cynically exploited, the money he made was invested in businesses that collapsed.

After the Second World War, Owens found a new role for himself, and his life picked up again when he worked for children's charities and went around the world as a goodwill ambassador for the United States. He died in 1980.

His friend and Olympic rival Lutz Long was killed in 1943, fighting with the German army in Sicily.

Rubble and strife in battlefield Beirut

In 1975, a civil war broke out in Lebanon when Christian and Muslim groups fought to decide who would have the most political power. Beirut, a city of many cultures and religions, was the main battleground, and the situation there soon became extremely complex. There were various competing factions, known as "militias", each with their own soldiers. Ten years later, in 1985, a British surgeon named Pauline Cutting took a job with the charity Medical Aid for Palestinians, and was sent to work in Beirut. This is her story.

On a dank December morning, a taxi bounced down a road strewn with debris and pockmarked with potholes. The route, between Beirut airport and its outer suburbs, ran parallel to open drains. The stench was appalling, but the passenger in the taxi, British surgeon Pauline Cutting, told herself she had better get used to it. She was experienced in accident and emergency work, and felt her expertise would be useful in Beirut. It was turning out to be far worse than she ever expected. A decade of civil war had ruined the once beautiful Mediterranean city, and 50,000 people had been killed. There seemed to be no solution to the savage fighting, which flared up or died down unpredictably.

The car passed a block of bomb-damaged apartments. One side had collapsed. Crumbling concrete floors and stairways hung precariously over the road, spilling out tangled wiring and seeping streams of water. The other side of the block was still occupied, and Cutting could see people peering uneasily from cracked or broken windows.

Deeper into the bustling city the buildings closed around the taxi in a maze of dark streets and dirty alleys. Clustered on corners were small groups of young men carrying machine guns and grenade launchers. Occasionally the sinister silhouette of a tank could be glimpsed, skulking behind a burned-out factory or lurking in a rubble-strewn side street. Chaos reigned. Here government had no control. There were no traffic signs, no policemen, no laws. Beirut was a battlefield.

❖

Cutting was taken to the Palestinian camp of Bourj al Barajneh. It was not really a camp as such, more a shanty town of tiny alleys. Once 30,000 people had lived here. By the time Cutting arrived, only 9,000 remained. Amid the alleys there were little shops selling food and clothes, hardware stores, and even a hairdresser and a garage.

In the middle of the camp was Haifa Hospital, a five-floor concrete building where Cutting would be in charge of the surgery department. When she arrived at the hospital, she was greeted warmly by a Palestinian doctor and taken on a tour of her new workplace. It was a dispiriting experience. Like all the other buildings in Bourj al Barajneh, it had been seriously damaged in the fighting. The top two floors had been so badly shelled they were beyond repair.

The entrance hall was littered with homeless families and their belongings, and children milled around the muddy floor. The hospital's most vital departments were sheltered in the relative safety of the basement. Here there was the emergency room, operating room, X-ray department and laboratory. Wards and staff living-quarters were scattered around the remaining inhabited floors.

Over the next few days, Cutting was introduced to the rest of the staff. There were six Palestinian doctors, 30 nurses (who worked in three shifts of 10), 10 office workers, and 10 cooks and cleaners. Cutting spent these first days in a daze, wondering if coming to Beirut had been a terrible mistake. Equipment was primitive and the staff felt demoralized, but she had so much responsibility and so much to learn, there was barely time to worry about it.

Most of her work involved treating day-to-day illnesses, and diseases caused by the camp's damp living conditions and dirty water. On top of this, there were the casualties of the war. Cutting was used to handling harrowing hospital cases such as car crash victims, and now she had to learn to deal with injuries caused by bombs, shells and bullets.

Working in the camp, Cutting also learned more about the plight of the Palestinians. Driven from their homeland following the creation of the state of Israel in 1947, they lived as refugees, unwanted and in great poverty, in nearby Arab states. Cutting had known little about this when she agreed to come to Beirut. After a few months at Haifa, she could see the difference her work made to the lives of the people she treated, and she became determined to stay and help.

But in early 1986, the situation in Beirut grew worse. Violence simmered among rival groups. Most troubling of all for Cutting were the kidnappings and murders of American or European residents. One United Nations worker was hanged, and his kidnappers released a video of his execution. Cutting saw the tape and was haunted by the fuzzy pictures of a hooded body swaying from a tree.

❖

But not everything was grim. Cutting made many friends during her stay, especially a Dutch nurse named Ben Alofs, who also worked in the camp. He was tall and amiable, and he seemed to know a lot about the complex politics of Beirut. Their friendship grew, and one day he gave her Ernest Hemmingway's *Farewell to Arms* – a novel about a passionate romance between an ambulance driver and nurse during World War One. It was something of a hint. Alofs was transferred to another part of the Lebanon soon after, and left a letter for Cutting saying he was falling in love with her.

It was around this time that Bourj al Barajneh began to be attacked again. The camp was surrounded by Amal militia men. Amal was one of several armed Muslim groups, and they wanted to drive the Palestinians from their city. Now, anyone venturing outside the camp could be kidnapped or killed. Inside Bourj al Barajneh, sniper fire and shelling became a daily danger.

On May 26, 1986, Amal soldiers stormed the camp. As the Palestinians fought to defend their territory, a steady stream of injured and dying men was brought into the hospital, and Cutting and her staff struggled to save the wounded. The following two days were just as difficult. As well as soldiers, children were also maimed in the fighting.

This was Cutting's first experience of all-out battlefield surgery. Apart from the daily danger of being killed, she had to make harrowing decisions about who to save and who to leave to die, and work with only the most basic supplies and equipment. There were no experts to consult, and no back-up facilities, and at times she felt very alone.

Worse was to come. On May 31, as Cutting lay asleep, a shell exploded above her room. The blast hit her like a punch in the chest, and thick black soot and rubble filled the hospital. The direct Amal attacks on Bourj al Barajneh had not succeeded, so instead they launched a week-long bombardment by tanks and artillery.

During this terrifying time, Cutting became good friends with two Belgian doctors who had also arrived at the hospital. They noticed how she read Ben Alofs' letter every time she lay down to sleep, and offered to teach her some Dutch, so she could speak to Ben in his own language.

At the end of June, after negotiations between the two sides, the shelling stopped. Government soldiers from Syria and Lebanon surrounded the camp, to prevent more attacks by Amal soldiers. For a while there was peace. There was other good news too. Ben Alofs was back in Beirut, working in another camp. Now Cutting was not so busy, she was able to spend time with him, and also travel to England for a break.

She returned to the camp in late August, to be joined soon afterwards by Scottish nurse Susie Wighton. Another round of fighting was brewing. The next few months were going to be very difficult.

Amal soldiers were still determined to drive the Palestinians from Beirut. At the end of October, they attacked Bourj al Barajneh and other Palestinian camps, in a campaign that became known as "The Camp War." Again, it became impossible for Palestinians to enter or leave Bourj al Barajneh. The fighting grew fiercer, and electricity to the camp was cut off. The hospital had to rely on diesel-powered generators. Hospital staff coped the best they could with ingenious improvisations. Headlight bulbs and batteries, for example, were removed from cars and rigged up to provide light in the darkened building.

During this ruthless campaign, the hospital became a target for the shelling. Sometimes direct hits shook the building to its foundations. When this happened, Cutting found herself trembling with fear. One shell explosion left her partially deaf for three weeks. Another shell shattered a water tank at the top of the building. Water trickled down the walls, collecting in deep pools in corridors and rooms throughout the hospital. On top of all their other troubles, the hospital staff had to cope with having constantly wet feet.

By mid-November, the Lebanese winter had taken hold. Cutting often worked 18 hours a day. In the rare moments she had to relax, she would fantasize about sitting in front of a burning coal fire, eating stew and dumplings. Ben Alofs, braving sniper fire and shells, and loaded with supplies of cakes and custard, crept into the camp whenever he could.

The bombardment increased, so staff moved their living quarters to the basement. They slept in a tiny room next to the operating surgery. It was warmer here, and everybody was friendly, but the strain of having no privacy was difficult to endure.

Despite the hardship, hospital staff still managed to work wonders. In November, a little boy was brought in with a terrible head wound. He was so disturbed that when anyone roused him he would cry like a cat. After a few days he started to speak, but would not open his eyes. Cutting was deeply moved by the courage that injured children showed. This boy had begun to learn English and, every morning when she visited, he would greet her with a formal "Good morning" and say, "I'm fine thank you." He went on to make a full recovery.

On another occasion, a Palestinian fighter was brought in close to death. Cutting and her team struggled all day to save him, removing 500 shell fragments from his body. He too survived. Successes like these strengthened Cutting's resolve to stay in the camp until the siege was over.

But the hospital was collapsing around them. Fuel was running out and the generators could only run for four hours at a time. In the cold, damp building the winter wind howled along corridors from one broken window to another, and black mildew crawled down the walls. To heat water, staff had to pour lighter fuel onto cotton on the stone floor and set it alight.

One of the men in the camp had worked in a filling station near to its perimeter. He began to wonder if a tunnel could be dug out to the fuel storage tanks that were built beneath the station. The idea was worth a try. A 40m (130ft) tunnel was carefully constructed. The burrowers did their job well. The tunnel went straight to the storage tanks and over 18,000 litres (4,000 gallons) were siphoned off. This escapade lifted everyone's spirits, solving at least one of the problems the camp faced.

The shortage of food just got worse. Cutting, along with everyone else, faced the winter months with a constant gnawing hunger, and sometimes she would faint while operating.

By the end of December, the third and fourth floor had collapsed under the shelling. The drainage and sanitation system had been destroyed, everyone had lice, garbage piled up in every corridor and rats scurried underfoot.

But there were still happy moments. January 19 was Cutting's birthday and Ben sneaked into the camp to present her with a siege survival kit – clean socks, soap, toothpaste, two candles and a packet of cigarettes. It was the best present she had ever had.

Cutting found the people of Bourj al Barajneh were exceptionally kind. Most days a little boy would bring her food from his family. When she said he was being too generous, he told her: "When we have a little, I will bring you a little. When we have nothing, then I will bring you nothing."

The camp was being starved and bombarded into submission. Worst of all was the fear that if Amal soldiers did break into Bourj al Barajneh, they might massacre its inhabitants. Palestinians had been slain in their thousands when rival militias had entered other refugee camps. Ben Alofs had nearly been killed himself when he had been caught up in such an attack. Cutting began to have terrible nightmares about these killings.

It seemed that nobody was prepared to help them. Intending to draw attention to the situation in the camp, Cutting, Ben Alofs and Susan Wighton prepared a formal statement to the international newspaper and broadcast journalists who were covering the fighting in Beirut. Their declaration, detailing the dreadful conditions of everyday life for Bourj al Barajneh's thousands of inhabitants, was transmitted over the hospital two-way radio.

Identifying themselves like this took a great deal of courage. They knew the American and European media would be more interested in the siege if they knew westerners were suffering too. But this also made them a target for Amal gunmen.

The declaration was broadcast on Arab radio stations, but it caused little international interest. The situation grew worse. Starvation in the camp became so bad that people were forced to eat rats, dogs, cats

– even grass. Their spirits at rock bottom, Cutting and her staff radioed out another declaration calling for the siege to be lifted. This time, the BBC World Service broadcast their statement.

Friday, February 13, was the worst day of the siege. A shell landed among a group of people who had ventured from their shelters. Many were terribly wounded. With the barest amount of equipment and supplies, the starving doctors operated on two patients at a time throughout the day.

As Cutting lay exhausted on her bed at 11:00 that night, she was roused by a message on the hospital radio. A BBC World Service reporter named Jim Muir, whose voice they all instantly recognized, was trying to contact her. Over a crackling radio link, they talked about conditions in the camp. Then, to Cutting's great surprise, her mother and father spoke to her. The BBC had arranged a radio link-up, so they could talk to their daughter. Muir came back on the radio and asked if they wanted to be rescued. Cutting was determined not to leave her patients. "I'm not coming out until it's finished," she replied.

After Jim Muir's report on the camp was broadcast, more journalists began to take an interest.

Cutting also learned that other militia groups in Beirut were beginning to side with the Palestinians against Amal. The increasing news coverage that followed their declarations had generated some support in Beirut for the camp's inhabitants.

On February 17, a cease-fire was negotiated and a few trucks full of food were allowed into the camp. Women were permitted to go out for a brief period each day to buy food. They were still shot at by snipers, and had to put up with brutal treatment by Amal forces. "We know all about Pauline Cutting and we are going to cut her to pieces," they told the women who passed through their checkpoints.

But now, television crews and newspaper journalists were frequent visitors to the camp. The plight of Bourj al Barajneh's inmates had become a focus for the world's media. On April 8, prompted by an international outcry, Syrian government troops came to patrol the perimeter. For the first time in five and a half months, there were no casualties admitted to the hospital. The International Red Cross arrived, along with new medical staff for the hospital. After 163 days the siege was truly over.

It was time to go home. After many sad farewells, Pauline Cutting, Ben Alofs and Susie Wighton made their way out of the camp. Cutting was still uneasy about Amal death threats, so at least 50 people surrounded her, to make sure she was not seized as she left. As she got into a waiting car, she turned to look back at the camp. All the hundreds of people who had come to see her off were smiling and waving. It was a heartbreaking sight. She was walking away. They had nowhere else to go.

The next day they took a ferry to Cyprus, where they were met by TV crews and journalists. All of a sudden the whole world wanted to know about these three medics from Bourj al Barajneh. In their hotel that evening they celebrated their survival with a bottle of wine, and entertained themselves by turning taps and lights on and off. It seemed unreal to be in a place where everything actually worked.

Afterwards

In 1987 Cutting was awarded an OBE (Order of the British Empire) by the British government, in recognition of her work in Bourj al Barajneh. She is a member of the board of Medical Aid for Palestinians, and returned to Beirut in October 1995, while reviewing the charity's projects in Lebanon.

After a spell in a hospital in Amsterdam, she now works in Ysbyty Gwynedd Accident and Emergency unit in North Wales. She is married to Ben Alofs, who has qualified as a doctor. They have two children.

Susie Wighton was awarded an MBE (Member of the British Empire) in 1987, and continued to work as an emergency relief worker in both Lebanon and Bosnia. She recently took a Master's Degree in community health, and now lives in Perthshire, where she works as a staff nurse. In 1999, the "Nursing Times" ran a cover story on her, with a special tribute from Cherie Blair (wife of Britain's Prime Minister).

Cosmonaut number one

In the dead of night, April 12, 1961, on a windswept plain in central Russia, a towering green rocket named *Vostok 1* sat pointing at the sky. Its task: to hurl a man into outer space. Airless and endless, home to lethal radiation, meteorite storms, and perils unknown to science, no deadlier environment ever awaited human exploration.

Technicians swarmed around the concrete launch pad, illuminated by powerful floodlights. Alongside *Vostok 1* rose huge steel gantries carrying fuel pipes and electricity cables which snaked into the rocket's thin metal casing. *Vostok 1* creaked and groaned as liquid oxygen and kerosene boiled away from access vents and into the cold night air.

As the first rays of the sun caught on the rocket's pointed tip, a small bus drew up beside it. Several figures emerged, including one dressed in a hefty orange protective suit and a large spherical helmet. The technicians stopped work for a moment as this man made a brief speech. As they began to applaud, he stiffly raised a hand to thank them.

Then he boarded an elevator, which took him to a small instrument-packed capsule at the top of the rocket. Here he was strapped into a couch, and 30 nuts were screwed in around an exit hatch to seal him in. One by one the technicians retired to the safety of nearby concrete bunkers, leaving him alone with his thoughts. Today would be a day of endless waiting.

The man cocooned in this tiny capsule was former jet fighter pilot Yuri Gagarin, officially known as "Cosmonaut number one." (The Russians called their spacemen "cosmonauts" – a word made up from *cosmos,* meaning "the universe", and *nautes*, a Greek word for "sailor".) Gagarin, an amiable 27 year-old, who was the son of a carpenter and a dairymaid, had been selected from over 3,000 volunteers to be the first man in space. No one on the project doubted he was the best person for the job. He was a cool and clear thinker, with great stamina and personal courage. If anyone was going to survive the hardships of space, Gagarin had the physical and mental ability to succeed.

Like the great European seafarers who had first explored the world's oceans three centuries before, he was venturing into the unknown. They had feared storms, sea monsters or savage tribes. The fears Gagarin faced were far stranger.

Space, as an environment, was extreme enough. But any visitor there also had to cope with the phenomenon of weightlessness. On Earth, gravity holds everything in its place. In space its effect is unnoticeable, and everything floats. In the years before Gagarin's journey, animals had been sent into orbit. The animals had coped well with weightlessness, but many scientists still wondered how a human would survive without gravity. Would blood still flow around his body? Would he choke on food? Worst of all, would his mind become so disoriented by this alien sensation that it would cease to function? (At the time it was a commonly held fear that space voyagers would return to Earth as burned-out zombies.)

There were other more obvious worries. To escape the pull of Earth's gravity, and place a capsule in orbit, *Vostok 1* needed to reach a speed of 40,000kmph (25,000mph). A cosmonaut would have to travel at speeds no human had experienced before. The physical damage this might cause could only be guessed at.

To reach this speed required a huge amount of fuel, and *Vostok 1*, like all rockets, was basically a huge fuel tank with a capsule on top. In the days before the Space Shuttle, rockets had several sections, known as stages, which would be discarded when the fuel inside them had been used up. *Vostok 1*, for example, had three stages.

Sending Vostok 1 into Space

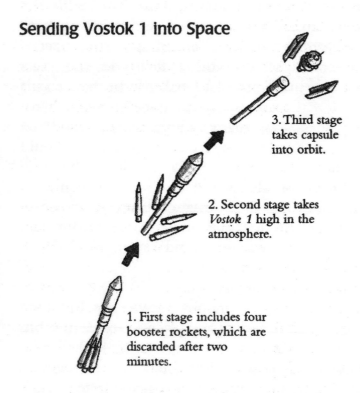

3. Third stage takes capsule into orbit.

2. Second stage takes *Vostok 1* high in the atmosphere.

1. First stage includes four booster rockets, which are discarded after two minutes.

The business of sending a vehicle into orbit by igniting thousands of tons of highly inflammable, explosive fuel was never going to make going into space particularly safe. Even today, over forty years later, space travel is still extremely dangerous. In

1961, rocket science was in its infancy, and the seven months prior to Gagarin's flight had seen some terrible disasters.

One rocket, aimed at the planet Mars, had blown up on the launch pad, killing Russia's space project director Marshall Mitrofan Nedelin and scores of his best technicians. More ominously still, several unmanned flights in the *Vostok*-type craft that Gagarin now sat inside had ended with the capsule locked in an endless orbit around the Earth, or burning up on its return through the atmosphere.

For three hours Gagarin sat waiting, as rocket engineers ran through final checks. Then, at 9:07am, it was time to go. Four metal gantries, which supported the rocket, unfolded, its engines ignited, and *Vostok 1* rose slowly into the air. In his capsule Gagarin heard a shrill whistle and then a mighty roar. As the rocket built up speed, he was pressed hard into his seat. After a minute the acceleration was so great he could barely move. Technicians on the ground, monitoring his physical reactions, noted his heart rate rise from its usual 64 beats a minute to 150.

After two minutes, the protective cover around the capsule was jettisoned and Gagarin could see out of the small portholes. The view of the Siberian landscape below was so stunning it took his mind off the unpleasant feeling of being squashed into his seat.

The crushing sensation began to lessen as *Vostok 1* gradually escaped the clutches of gravity, and entered into orbit. Only minutes after take off, Gagarin was flying around the Earth at an incredible speed: around 8km (5 miles) a second.

The first thing he noticed was how he had begun to rise in his chair as far as his harness would allow. He was the first human being to experience the sensation of weightlessness. Initially he found it unpleasant, but adapted very quickly. It was not nearly as uncomfortable as scientists had predicted. Gagarin unbuckled his belt and hung in the air. It felt as though his arms and legs did not belong to him, and his map case, pencil and notepad floated by. The whole sensation was very dreamlike. Strangest of all, he noticed, was the way in which liquids behaved. Water leaking from a drink container formed into a sphere and floated in mid-air until it reached a solid surface where it settled like dew on a flower.

Now he was safely in space, the Soviet authorities decided to release the news to an unsuspecting world. Radio Moscow interrupted its usual schedule with a burst of patriotic music and a solemn voice which announced: "The world's first spaceship with a man on board has been launched in the Soviet

Union on a round-the-world orbit."Throughout the country, factory, farm and office workers listened intently, immensely proud of the fact that their country could perform such a scientific miracle.

Vostok 1

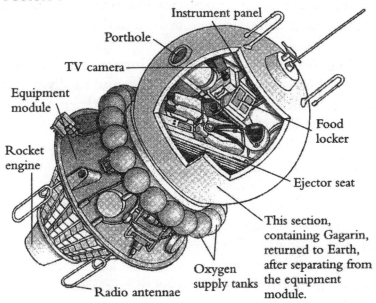

Instrument panel

Porthole

TV camera

Equipment module

Rocket engine

Food locker

Ejector seat

This section, containing Gagarin, returned to Earth, after separating from the equipment module.

Oxygen supply tanks

Radio antennae

There was very little actual flying to be done. Flight corrections were made automatically. The discarding of stages, the flight-path of the capsule, the speed it moved, even the conditions inside the cabin, were all controlled from the ground, or by computer. This left Gagarin free to concentrate on what he saw and felt. He quickly realized that weightlessness was not going to affect the way he worked, so he began to jot down his observations and report what he could see.

The orbit of *Vostok 1* took it between 181km (112 miles) and 327km (203 miles) above the surface of the Earth. From here, coastlines, mountain ranges and forests could easily be seen, as well as the curve of the Earth itself. Along this curve, the pale blue atmosphere gradually darkened into a series of rich shades – from turquoise, blue, violet and finally black. Above this beautiful sight hung the dark eternity of space. For Gagarin, who had been brought up on a farm, space looked like "a huge black field sown with star-like grain".

The Sun looked very different. Without Earth's atmosphere to soften its rays, it seemed a hundred times brighter. It reminded Gagarin of molten metal, and when it shone directly into his capsule he had to shield his portholes with protective filters.

Suddenly, *Vostok 1* plunged into pitch dark as the capsule flew from the rays of the Sun and into the Earth's shadow. Below him, Gagarin could see only blackness, but quickly realized he must be flying over an ocean.

Although the cosmonaut was neither hungry nor thirsty, he ate a small meal – carefully sucking pulped food from a tube-like container, and drinking a little water. He had to be careful about transferring both food and liquid from the containers to his mouth, in case any floated off and became attached to his instrument panels.

Soon *Vostok 1* emerged again into the light, the horizon blazing from bright orange through all the shades of the rainbow.

Gagarin's mind began to wander. He thought of the bustling streets of Moscow, where he had visited his wife and two daughters a couple of days before the flight. But in less than 90 minutes *Vostok I* had orbited the entire Earth, and now it was time to return. This was the most dangerous part of the flight. If something had gone wrong at take-off, Gagarin had at least a small chance of ejecting to safety. If anything went wrong now, the first man in space could be marooned forever or burned to a cinder. Until this time, Gagarin had had every faith in his spacecraft, but now, in the most dangerous part of his trip, he began to wonder if it would work properly.

On-board equipment placed the capsule in the correct flight path, using the Sun as a guide, and *Vostok I* began its giddy descent. As it plunged down into the upper layers of the atmosphere, the outer skin of the craft began to glow red–hot. Fiery crimson flames licked along the heat–shield underneath the capsule, and flashed past his small portholes. Gagarin was once again pinned to his seat. Coming back was much more unpleasant than going out, and when his ship began to tumble around he became immensely worried.

Things had in fact gone seriously wrong. Before re-entry, his small capsule was supposed to separate from a connected equipment module. What Gagarin did not realize was that this had not happened properly, and both craft were still tethered to each other by electrical wiring. Fortunately the heat of re-entry burned away the wire cables. The two craft separated and disaster was averted.

When the equipment module broke free from Gagarin's capsule, the tumbling finally stopped, and descent parachutes opened to slow down the speeding capsule. As soon as this had happened, Gagarin realized that the most hazardous part of his journey was finally over. He had taken an enormous risk on his life for the glory of his country and now he was going to live to tell this extraordinary tale. Overcome with sheer relief, he began to sing at the top of his voice.

There was still one final, dangerous step to take. 6,000m (20,000ft) from the ground, Gagarin braced himself in his seat and was ejected from the capsule. Once outside *Vostok 1* he floated back to Earth by parachute. Soviet rocket engineers thought that landing inside the capsule would be too jarring, and that parachuting down separately would be safer.

Around the world in 108 minutes

Vostok 1 made a single orbit before returning to Earth.

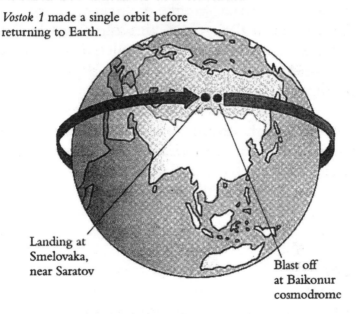

Landing at Smelovaka, near Saratov

Blast off at Baikonur cosmodrome

At 10:55am, less than two hours after he had taken off, Gagarin landed in a field near the village of Smelovka, watched by two startled farm workers. They walked toward him, anxious to help, but slowed uncertainly as they approached. His unusual, bright orange spacesuit, and large white helmet, clearly frightened them. One, a woman named Anna Takhtarova, asked: "Are you from outer space?"

Gagarin took off his helmet, to show the farm workers he was a man and not an alien. He reassured Takhtarova that he was a fellow Russian, but yes, indeed, he had come from outer space. Then other farm workers arrived. Unlike Takhtarova, they had been listening to their radio. "It's Yuri Gagarin! It's Yuri Gagarin!" one shouted, completely astonished to be meeting the remarkable man he had heard about minutes before.

Gagarin and the excited farm workers embraced and kissed like long-lost relatives. This was indeed an extraordinary moment. For the first time in history, a man had left the planet and returned safely to Earth.

Afterwards

In 1961 space exploration was a matter of intense rivalry between nations. The communist Soviet Union (now Russia) and capitalist United States vied with each other to demonstrate their technological superiority to the world. There was great competition to see who would be the first to put a man into orbit, as this would be a good advertisement for each nation.

On his return Gagarin was declared a "Hero of the Soviet Union". His 1961 space flight made him an instant global celebrity, and he spent the next five years touring the world, even visiting the Soviet Union's arch-rival, the United States. He was an excellent ambassador for his country, and his amiable modesty made him hugely popular with the thousands who turned out to see him.

In 1968 he began to train for another space flight, but was killed when a jet he was flying swerved to miss another aircraft and hit the ground. A massive funeral ceremony was held in Moscow, but only in 1984 did the Soviet authorities reveal that Gagarin's body had never been found.

Death or glory for the "last gladiator"

There never was a hero quite like Robert "Evel" Knievel – the world's most famous motorcycle stuntman. Knievel (pronounced Kuh-nee-val) was a self-made legend from the top of his cracked skull to the bottom of his broken toes. By 1974, 10 years of jumping across snake pits, lion cages, fountains and rows of trucks had brought Evel a Rolls-Royce, half a million dollars a year, and a reputation as one of America's most swashbuckling celebrities.

The stories they told... how he was a reformed bank robber, how he'd broken every bone in his body, how he washed down painkillers with his own "Montana Mary" cocktail of beer, tomato juice, whiskey and engine oil...

Well, some of it was true. Knievel hadn't broken *every* bone in his body, just 35 of them. One jump had put him in a coma for 29 days. 14 major operations had left him with one leg shorter than the other, and his body was held together with steel plates and screws. Once, when quizzed by a reporter who asked him why he did it, he swaggered, "I'm a competitor. I face the greatest competition any man can face, and that, my friend, is death."

But Knievel was married with three children. He was growing weary of his "death or glory" lifestyle. Still, there was one final challenge the great competitor had yet to face. For years he had dreamed of hurtling up a ramp at full throttle, and sailing clean across the Arizona Grand Canyon. It was a perfect spot – a national landmark and the greatest chasm on the face of the Earth. But the Navaho Indians, who owned the land, considered it sacred, and would have nothing to do with Knievel. Even $40,000 wouldn't make them change their minds. The Snake River canyon in Idaho was chosen instead. It was 1.6km (1 mile) across, and its dark, jagged walls made it a suitably sinister spot for Knievel's last stand.

A former rocket engineer was hired to design a vehicle to cross it. He presented Knievel with the *Sky Cycle*. It may have been called a cycle, but it was actually one million dollars worth of steam-powered rocket. The plan was simple. Knievel would sit in the rocket, and be fired up a ramp and over the gaping mouth of the canyon. Once across, a parachute would slow the *Sky Cycle* to a safe landing speed. The day was set for September 8, 1974, and Knievel played up the stunt for all it was worth. He told reporters he would survive "... if the heater doesn't blow up and scald me to death, if the *Sky Cycle* goes straight up and doesn't flip over backwards, if I reach 3,000ft, if the parachute opens, and if I don't hit the canyon wall at 300mph."

Within weeks the event had captured the imagination of the world. Fifteen businesses invested in it. There were toys, T-shirts, records, even silver and gold commemorative statues. As the day drew near, 50,000 spectators gathered at the Snake River site, paying a hefty $25 a ticket. Most lucrative of all was the plan to broadcast the action to several million paying customers in movie houses throughout the world. Knievel's fans called him "the last gladiator", and many believed he was actually going to die. According to his publicity men, his jump would most likely "leave behind the richest widow in America".

But to others, the stunt was a con. A bright teenager, they said, could have calculated the rocket's flight path, and see that it would land perfectly safely. One cynic, regarding the mob of desperado bikers who made up the bulk of the Snake River audience, suggested that the crowd was more dangerous than the *Sky Cycle*. Even the man himself was unsure... "I don't know if I'm an athlete, a daredevil, a promoter, a hoax, or just a nut."

So it was, on the afternoon of September 8, 1974, that Evel Knievel mounted his *Sky Cycle* and launched himself into the clean blue sky. The omens were not good. Two test runs had seen unmanned *Sky Cycles* crash into the canyon's far wall. Showing uncommon courage, Knievel was undeterred. Just before the jump he told reporters he'd "spit the canyon wall in the eye just before I hit."

He was right to expect the worst. As the rocket sped up the launch ramp, a parachute accidentally opened behind the steam-powered thruster. The flight of the *Sky Cycle* was now fatally flawed, and it lurched into the canyon, parachute billowing behind. Knievel, struggling to escape, could not free himself in time to jump to safety. The *Sky Cycle* grazed the craggy wall of the canyon, and then dumped the hapless stunt man in the Snake River.

Quickly rescued, Knievel was shaken but uninjured. His stunt had turned out to be hair-raisingly dangerous after all, and there was worse to come. Disappointed by his poor performance, sections of the crowd rioted. They stormed the press enclosure and had to be beaten off by policemen. But injured pride was a small price to pay. On that day, Knievel's dare-devil heroism had captured the imagination of the world and made him around five million dollars. Even today, Knievel Web sites are full of messages from adoring fans, while Knievel's own official Web site still does a lucrative trade in toys and other memorabilia.

TRUE
SPY
STORIES

Paul Dowswell

"In all your years of fame," Kramer explained delicately, "you have known some of the most powerful men in Europe. Would you consider returning to Paris now to mingle again with these influential gentlemen? And, while you're doing this, might you be able to keep me informed of anything interesting they might say?"

Margaretha looked curious but non-committal.

Kramer went on, "We could pay you well for this information — say 24,000 francs."

What are real spies like? Some, like beautiful Mata Hari, are every bit as glamorous as famous fictional agents such as James Bond. But spies usually live shadowy double lives, risking prison, torture and execution for a chance to change history.

Also from Usborne True Stories

TRUE
ESCAPE
STORIES

Paul Dowswell

Finally, the night had come to take a
trip to the roof. Morris spent the day
beforehand trying to curb his
restlessness. What if the way up to the
roof was blocked? What if the ventilator
motor had been replaced after all? All
their painstaking work would be
wasted. The 12 year sentence stretched
out before him. Then another awful
thought occurred. The holes in the wall
would be discovered eventually, and
that would mean even more years
added on to his sentence.

As well as locked doors, high walls and barbed wire,
many escaping prisoners also face savage dogs and
armed guards who shoot to kill. From Alcatraz to
Devil's Island, read the extraordinary tales of people
who risked their lives for their freedom.

TRUE SURVIVAL STORIES

Paul Dowswell

As he fell through the floor Griffiths instinctively grabbed at the bombsight with both hands, but an immense gust of freezing air sucked the rest of his body out of the aircraft. With the wind and the throb of the Boston's two engines roaring in his ears, he found himself halfway out of the plane, legs and lower body pressed hard against the fuselage. He yelled at the top of his voice: "Geeeerrrrooooowwww!!!!", but knew immediately that there was almost no chance his crewmate could hear him.

From shark attacks and blazing airships to exploding spacecraft and sinking submarines, these are real stories of people who have stared death in the face and lived to tell the tale. Find out what separates the living from the dead when catastrophe strikes.